MznLnx

Missing Links Exam Preps

Exam Prep for

Personal Finance

Rosefsky, 8th Edition

The MznLnx Exam Prep is your link from the texbook and lecture to your exams.
The MznLnx Exam Preps are unauthorized and comprehensive reviews of your textbooks.

All material provided by MznLnx and Rico Publications (c) 2010
Textbook publishers and textbook authors do not particpate in or contribute to these reviews.

MznLnx

Rico Publications

Exam Prep for Personal Finance
8th Edition
Rosefsky

Publisher: Raymond Houge
Assistant Editor: Michael Rouger
Text and Cover Designer: Lisa Buckner
Marketing Manager: Sara Swagger
Project Manager, Editorial Production: Jerry Emerson
Art Director: Vernon Lowerui

Product Manager: Dave Mason
Editorial Assitant: Rachel Guzmanji
Pedagogy: Debra Long
Cover Image: Jim Reed/Getty Images
Text and Cover Printer: City Printing, Inc.
Compositor: Media Mix, Inc.

(c) 2010 Rico Publications

ALL RIGHTS RESERVED. No part of this work covered by the copyright may be reproduced or used in any form or by an means--graphic, electronic, or mechanical, including photocopying, recording, taping, Web distribution, information storage, and retrieval systems, or in any other manner--without the written permission of the publisher.

Printed in the United States
ISBN:

For more information about our products, contact us at:
Dave.Mason@RicoPublications.com

For permission to use material from this text or product, submit a request online to:
Dave.Mason@RicoPublications.com

Contents

CHAPTER 1
The Economy: How It Works and What It Means to You — 1

CHAPTER 2
Working, Planning, and Budgeting — 5

CHAPTER 3
Sensible Shopping and Spending — 13

CHAPTER 4
Frauds and Swindles and How to Avoid Them — 16

CHAPTER 5
Transportation: Buying, Financing, and Insuring Your Cars — 20

CHAPTER 6
Buying a Home — 24

CHAPTER 7
Financing a Home — 30

CHAPTER 8
Housing Costs and Regulations — 39

CHAPTER 9
Renting — 43

CHAPTER 10
Selling Your Home — 47

CHAPTER 11
Financial Institutions — 50

CHAPTER 12
Credit and Borrowing — 57

CHAPTER 13
Making Your Money Grow: An Overview — 64

CHAPTER 14
Making Your Money Grow: The Money Market — 72

CHAPTER 15
Making Your Money Grow: The Stock Market — 83

CHAPTER 16
Making Your Money Grow: Real Estate and Other Opportunities — 98

CHAPTER 17
Life, Health, and Income Insurance — 107

CHAPTER 18
Financial Plannina for Later Years — 113

CHAPTER 19
Estate Planning — 119

CHAPTER 20
Income Taxes — 122

Contents (Cont.)

CHAPTER 21
  Working for Yourself   125
ANSWER KEY   128

TO THE STUDENT

COMPREHENSIVE

The *MznLnx* Exam Prep series is designed to help you pass your exams. Editors at MznLnx review your textbooks and then prepare these practice exams to help you master the textbook material. Unlike study guides, workbooks, and practice tests provided by the texbook publisher and textbook authors, *MznLnx* gives you **all** of the material in each chapter in exam form, not just samples, so you can be sure to nail your exam.

MECHANICAL

The MznLnx Exam Prep series creates exams that will help you learn the subject matter as well as test you on your understanding. Each question is designed to help you master the concept. Just working through the exams, you gain an understanding of the subject--its a simple mechanical process that produces success.

INTEGRATED STUDY GUIDE AND REVIEW

MznLnx is not just a set of exams designed to test you, its also a comprehensive review of the subject content. Each exam question is also a review of the concept, making sure that you will get the answer correct without having to go to other sources of material. You learn as you go! Its the easiest way to pass an exam.

HUMOR

Studying can be tedious and dry. MznLnx's instructional design includes moderate humor within the exam questions on occassion, to break the tedium and revitalize the brain

Chapter 1. The Economy: How It Works and What It Means to You

1. _____ is an economic model based on price, utility and quantity in a market. It predicts that in a competitive market, price will function to equalize the quantity demanded by consumers, and the quantity supplied by producers, resulting in an economic equilibrium of price and quantity. Similarly, an increase in the number of workers tends to result in lower wages and vice-versa.

   a. Price channel
   b. Rural credit cooperatives
   c. Supply and demand
   d. Loan participation

2. The phrase _____ according to the Organization for Economic Co-operation and Development, refers to 'creative work undertaken on a systematic basis in order to increase the stock of knowledge, including knowledge of (hu)man, culture and society, and the use of this stock of knowledge to devise new applications'.

   New product design and development is more than often a crucial factor in the survival of a company. In an industry that is fast changing, firms must continually revise their design and range of products. This is necessary due to continuous technology change and development as well as other competitors and the changing preference of customers.

   a. 7-Eleven
   b. 4-4-5 Calendar
   c. 529 plan
   d. Research and development

3. _____ refers to government attempts to influence the direction of the economy through changes in government taxes, or through some spending (fiscal allowances.)

   _____ can be contrasted with the other main type of economic policy, monetary policy, which attempts to stabilize the economy by controlling interest rates and the supply of money. The two main instruments of _____ are government spending and taxation.

   a. Qualified residence interest
   b. Tax incidence
   c. Fiscal policy
   d. Tax exemption

4. _____ is the process by which the government, or monetary authority of a country controls (i) the supply of money central bank (ii) availability of money, and (iii) cost of money or rate of interest, in order to attain a set of objectives oriented towards the growth and stability of the economy. Monetary theory provides insight into how to craft optimal _____.

   _____ is referred to as either being an expansionary policy where an expansionary policy increases the total supply of money in the economy, and a contractionary policy decreases the total money supply.

Chapter 1. The Economy: How It Works and What It Means to You

   a. Natural resources consumption tax
   b. Tax exemption
   c. Monetary policy
   d. Federal Open Market Committee

5. _____ established the Federal Deposit Insurance Corporation (FDIC) in the United States and included banking reforms, some of which were designed to control speculation. Some provisions such as Regulation Q, which allowed the Federal Reserve to regulate interest rates in savings accounts, were repealed by the Depository Institutions Deregulation and Monetary Control Act of 1980. Provisions that prohibit a bank holding company from owning other financial companies were repealed on November 12, 1999, by the Gramm-Leach-Bliley Act.
   a. Comanity
   b. The Glass-Steagall Act of 1933
   c. Shell Creation Group
   d. BootStrap Method

6. The _____ is an important selective, mainly private, international organization designed by its founders to supervise and liberalize international trade. The organization officially commenced on 1 January 1995, under the Marrakesh Agreement, succeeding the 1947 General Agreement on Tariffs and Trade (GATT.)

The _____ deals with regulation of trade between participating countries; it provides a framework for negotiating and formalising trade agreements, and a dispute resolution process aimed at enforcing participants' adherence to _____ agreements which are signed by representatives of member governments and ratified by their parliaments.

   a. Financial Crimes Enforcement Network
   b. Public Company Accounting Oversight Board
   c. Gamelan Council
   d. World Trade Organization

7. _____ are legal property rights over creations of the mind, both artistic and commercial, and the corresponding fields of law. Under _____ law, owners are granted certain exclusive rights to a variety of intangible assets, such as musical, literary, and artistic works; ideas, discoveries and inventions; and words, phrases, symbols, and designs. Common types of _____ include copyrights, trademarks, patents, industrial design rights and trade secrets.
   a. A Random Walk Down Wall Street
   b. Intellectual property
   c. ABN Amro
   d. AAB

Chapter 1. The Economy: How It Works and What It Means to You

8. _____ measures the nominal future sum of money that a given sum of money is 'worth' at a specified time in the future assuming a certain interest rate rate of return; it is the present value multiplied by the accumulation function.

The value does not include corrections for inflation or other factors that affect the true value of money in the future. This is used in time value of money calculations.

   a. Present value of costs
   b. Discounted cash flow
   c. Future-oriented
   d. Future value

9. _____ is a mathematical science pertaining to the collection, analysis, interpretation or explanation, and presentation of data. It also provides tools for prediction and forecasting based on data. It is applicable to a wide variety of academic disciplines, from the natural and social sciences to the humanities, government and business.
   a. Sample size
   b. Mean
   c. Covariance
   d. Statistics

10. The term _____ describes two different concepts:

    - The first is a recognition of partial payment already made towards taxes due.
    - The second is a state benefit paid to workers through the tax system, which has the effect of increasing (rather than reducing) net income.

Within the Australian, Canadian, United Kingdom, and United States tax systems, a _____ is a recognition of partial payment already made towards taxes due. A similar concept exists (fr:Avoir fiscal) in the French tax system. This situation arises, for example, when standard rate tax has been deducted at source , but the tax-payer is subject to further taxation at a higher rate. It also applies in dividend imputation systems.

   a. 4-4-5 Calendar
   b. Tax credit
   c. 529 plan
   d. 7-Eleven

11. _____ is the provision of resources (such as granting a loan) by one party to another party where that second party does not reimburse the first party immediately, thereby generating a debt, and instead arranges either to repay or return those resources (or material(s) of equal value) at a later date. The first party is called a creditor, also known as a lender, while the second party is called a debtor, also known as a borrower.

Movements of financial capital are normally dependent on either _____ or equity transfers.

a. Clearing house
b. Comparable
c. Warrant
d. Credit

12. In economics, _____ is a rise in the general level of prices of goods and services in an economy over a period of time. The term '_____' once referred to increases in the money supply (monetary _____); however, economic debates about the relationship between money supply and price levels have led to its primary use today in describing price _____. _____ can also be described as a decline in the real value of money--a loss of purchasing power in the medium of exchange which is also the monetary unit of account.

a. AAB
b. ABN Amro
c. A Random Walk Down Wall Street
d. Inflation

13. In economics, business, and accounting, a _____ is the value of money that has been used up to produce something, and hence is not available for use anymore. In business, the _____ may be one of acquisition, in which case the amount of money expended to acquire it is counted as _____. In this case, money is the input that is gone in order to acquire the thing.

a. Fixed costs
b. Sliding scale fees
c. Marginal cost
d. Cost

14. _____ are costs incurred on the purchase of land, buildings, construction and equipment to be used in the production of goods or the rendering of services. In other words, the total cost needed to bring a project to a commercially operable status. However, _____ are not limited to the initial construction of a factory or other business.

a. Trade-off
b. Defined contribution plan
c. Capital outflow
d. Capital costs

Chapter 2. Working, Planning, and Budgeting

1. In economics, a _____ is a general slowdown in economic activity in a country over a sustained period of time, or a business cycle contraction. During _____s, many macroeconomic indicators vary in a similar way. Production as measured by Gross Domestic Product (GDP), employment, investment spending, capacity utilization, household incomes and business profits all fall during _____s.
   a. Mercantilism
   b. Fixed exchange rate
   c. Behavioral finance
   d. Recession

2. _____ is a type of trade policy that allows traders to act and transact without interference from government. Thus, the policy permits trading partners mutual gains from trade, with goods and services produced according to the theory of comparative advantage.

   Under a _____ policy, prices are a reflection of true supply and demand, and are the sole determinant of resource allocation.

   a. Monte Carlo methods
   b. Seasoned equity offering
   c. Yield spread
   d. Free Trade

3. _____ and benefits in kind are various non-wage compensations provided to employees in addition to their normal wages or salaries. Where an employee exchanges (cash) wages for some other form of benefit, this is generally referred to as a 'salary sacrifice' arrangement. In most countries, most kinds of _____ are taxable to at least some degree.
   a. ABN Amro
   b. AAB
   c. A Random Walk Down Wall Street
   d. Employee benefits

4. The _____ is a trilateral trade bloc in North America created by the governments of the United States, Canada, and Mexico. The agreement creating the trade bloc came into force on January 1, 1994. It superseded the Canada-United States Free Trade Agreement between the U.S. and Canada.
   a. 4-4-5 Calendar
   b. 529 plan
   c. 7-Eleven
   d. North American Free Trade Agreement

5. In law, _____ is to give an immediately secured right of present or future enjoyment. One has a vested right to an asset that cannot be taken away by any third party, even though one may not yet possess the asset. When the right, interest or title to the present or future possession of a legal estate can be transferred to any other party, it is termed a vested interest.
   a. Competition law
   b. Limited liability
   c. Vesting
   d. Corporate governance

6. _____, in bookkeeping, refers to assets, liabilities, income, and expenses recorded on individual pages of the so called book of final entry or ledger. Changes in _____ value are made by chronologically posting debit (DR) and credit (CR) entries to its page. Examples of _____s are cash, _____s receivable, mortgages, loans, land and buildings, common stock, sales, services provided, wages, and payroll overhead.
   a. Account
   b. Accretion
   c. Alpha
   d. Option

7. An _____ is a contract written by a seller that conveys to the buyer the right -- but not the obligation -- to buy (in the case of a call _____) or to sell (in the case of a put _____) a particular asset, such as a piece of property such as, among others, a futures contract. In return for granting the _____, the seller collects a payment (the premium) from the buyer.

For example, buying a call _____ provides the right to buy a specified quantity of a security at a set strike price at some time on or before expiration, while buying a put _____ provides the right to sell.

   a. Annuity
   b. AT'T Mobility LLC
   c. Amortization
   d. Option

8. _____, refers to consumption opportunity gained by an entity within a specified time frame, which is generally expressed in monetary terms. However, for households and individuals, '_____ is the sum of all the wages, salaries, profits, interests payments, rents and other forms of earnings received... in a given period of time.' For firms, _____ generally refers to net-profit: what remains of revenue after expenses have been subtracted.
   a. OIBDA
   b. Accrual
   c. Annual report
   d. Income

Chapter 2. Working, Planning, and Budgeting

9. The _____ of 1974 (Pub.L. 93-406, 88 Stat. 829, enacted September 2, 1974) is an American federal statute that establishes minimum standards for pension plans in private industry and provides for extensive rules on the federal income tax effects of transactions associated with employee benefit plans.

    a. Employee Retirement Income Security Act
    b. Expedited Funds Availability Act
    c. Express warranty
    d. Articles of Partnership

10. A _____ is a fungible, negotiable instrument representing financial value. They are broadly categorized into debt securities (such as banknotes, bonds and debentures), and equity securities; e.g., common stocks. The company or other entity issuing the _____ is called the issuer.

    a. Security
    b. Book entry
    c. Securities lending
    d. Tracking stock

11. The _____ of 1967, Pub. L. No. 90-202, 81 Stat. 602 (Dec. 15, 1967), codified as Chapter 14 of Title 29 of the United States Code, 29 U.S.C. § 621 through 29 U.S.C. § 634 (ADEA), prohibits employment discrimination against persons 40 years of age or older in the United States). The law also sets standards for pensions and benefits provided by employers and requires that information about the needs of older workers be provided to the general public.

    a. ABN Amro
    b. Age Discrimination in Employment Act
    c. A Random Walk Down Wall Street
    d. AAB

12. The _____ of 1938 also called the Wages and Hours Bill, is United States federal law that applies to employees engaged in interstate commerce or employed by an enterprise engaged in commerce or in the production of goods for commerce, unless the employer can claim an exemption from coverage. The _____ established a national minimum wage, guaranteed time and a half for overtime in certain jobs, and prohibited most employment of minors in 'oppressive child labor,' a term defined in the statute.

    a. Duty of loyalty
    b. Fair Labor Standards Act
    c. Companies law
    d. Bundesrechnungshof

Chapter 2. Working, Planning, and Budgeting

13. The _____ of 1990 (ADA) is the short title of United States (Pub.L. 101-336, 104 Stat. 327, enacted July 26, 1990), codified at 42 U.S.C.§ 12101 et seq. It was signed into law on July 26, 1990, by President George H. W. Bush, and later amended with changes effective January 1, 2009. The _____ is a wide-ranging civil rights law that prohibits, under certain circumstances, discrimination based on disability. It affords similar protections against discrimination to Americans with disabilities as the Civil Rights Act of 1964.

    a. A Random Walk Down Wall Street
    b. ABN Amro
    c. AAB
    d. Americans with Disabilities Act

14. The _____ of 1993 (Pub.L. 103-3, enacted February 5, 1993) is a United States labor law allowing an employee to take unpaid leave due to a serious health condition that makes the employee unable to perform his job or to care for a sick family member or to care for a new son or daughter (including by birth, adoption or foster care.) The bill was among the first signed into law by President Bill Clinton in his first term.

    a. Federal Acquisition Regulations
    b. Royalties
    c. Pre-emption right
    d. Family and Medical Leave Act

15. _____ is the provision of resources (such as granting a loan) by one party to another party where that second party does not reimburse the first party immediately, thereby generating a debt, and instead arranges either to repay or return those resources (or material(s) of equal value) at a later date. The first party is called a creditor, also known as a lender, while the second party is called a debtor, also known as a borrower.

    Movements of financial capital are normally dependent on either _____ or equity transfers.

    a. Comparable
    b. Warrant
    c. Credit
    d. Clearing house

16. A _____ is a means of collecting a monetary judgment against a defendant by ordering a third party (the garnishee) to pay money, otherwise owed to the defendant, directly to the plaintiff.

    Wage _____, the most common type of _____, is the process of deducting money from an employee's monetary compensation (including salary) as a result of a court order. In the United States, such payments are limited by federal law to 25 percent of the disposable income that the employee earns.

Chapter 2. Working, Planning, and Budgeting

a. FTSE MTIRS Indices
b. Gordon growth model
c. Floor broker
d. Garnishment

17. The _____ is a 1935 United States federal law that protects the rights of most workers in the private sector to organize labor unions, to engage in collective bargaining, and to take part in strikes and other forms of concerted activity in support of their demands. The Act does not, on the other hand, cover those workers who are covered by the Railway Labor Act, agricultural employees, domestic employees, supervisors, independent contractors and some close relatives of individual employers.

It was in a context of severe economic troubles that the Wagner Act came into effect.

a. Global depository receipt
b. National Labor Relations Act
c. Controlled foreign corporations
d. Certified Emission Reductions

18. A _____ is an exchange of promises between two or more parties to do an act which is enforceable in a court of law. It is where an unqualified offer meets a qualified acceptance and the parties reach Consensus ad Idem. The parties must have the necessary capacity to _____ and the _____ must not be either trifling, indeterminate, impossible or illegal.

a. 7-Eleven
b. Contract
c. 4-4-5 Calendar
d. 529 plan

19. _____ or financing is to provide capital (funds), which means money for a project, a person, a business or any other private or public institutions.

Those funds can be allocated for either short term or long term purposes. The health fund is a new way of _____ private healthcare centers.

a. Proxy fight
b. Product life cycle
c. Synthetic CDO
d. Funding

Chapter 2. Working, Planning, and Budgeting

20. _____ is the discipline of identifying, monitoring and limiting risks. In some cases the acceptable risk may be near zero. Risks can come from accidents, natural causes and disasters as well as deliberate attacks from an adversary.
   a. Penny stock
   b. 4-4-5 Calendar
   c. FIFO
   d. Risk management

21. In economics, business, and accounting, a _____ is the value of money that has been used up to produce something, and hence is not available for use anymore. In business, the _____ may be one of acquisition, in which case the amount of money expended to acquire it is counted as _____. In this case, money is the input that is gone in order to acquire the thing.
   a. Fixed costs
   b. Cost
   c. Sliding scale fees
   d. Marginal cost

22. _____ measures the nominal future sum of money that a given sum of money is 'worth' at a specified time in the future assuming a certain interest rate rate of return; it is the present value multiplied by the accumulation function.

The value does not include corrections for inflation or other factors that affect the true value of money in the future. This is used in time value of money calculations.

   a. Future-oriented
   b. Future value
   c. Present value of costs
   d. Discounted cash flow

23. _____ are formal records of a business' financial activities.

Chapter 2. Working, Planning, and Budgeting

_____ provide an overview of a business' financial condition in both short and long term. There are four basic _____:

1. **Balance sheet**: also referred to as statement of financial position or condition, reports on a company's assets, liabilities, and net equity as of a given point in time.
2. **Income statement**: also referred to as Profit and Loss statement (or a 'P'L'), reports on a company's income, expenses, and profits over a period of time.
3. **Statement of retained earnings**: explains the changes in a company's retained earnings over the reporting period.
4. **Statement of cash flows**: reports on a company's cash flow activities, particularly its operating, investing and financing activities.

a. Financial statements
b. Notes to the Financial Statements
c. Statement of retained earnings
d. Statement on Auditing Standards No. 70: Service Organizations

24. In business and accounting, _____s are everything of value that is owned by a person or company. The balance sheet of a firm records the monetary value of the _____s owned by the firm. The two major _____ classes are tangible _____s and intangible _____s.
   a. EBITDA
   b. Income
   c. Accounts payable
   d. Asset

25. In business, _____ is the total assets minus total outside liabilities of an individual or a company. For a company, this is called shareholders' equity and may be referred to as book value. _____ is stated as at a particular point in time.
   a. Moneylender
   b. Certified International Investment Analyst
   c. Restructuring
   d. Net worth

26. _____ is the process of disposing of an estate. _____ typically attempts to eliminate uncertainties over the administration of a probate and maximize the value of the estate by reducing taxes and other expenses. Guardians are often designated for minor children and beneficiaries in incapacity.

Chapter 2. Working, Planning, and Budgeting

a. ABN Amro
b. A Random Walk Down Wall Street
c. AAB
d. Estate planning

27. _____ is the income of individuals or nations after adjusting for inflation. It is calculated by subtracting inflation from the nominal income. Real variables, such as _____, real GDP, and real interest rate are variables that are measured in physical units, while nominal variables such as nominal income, nominal GDP, and nominal interest rate are measured in monetary units.
    a. 529 plan
    b. 7-Eleven
    c. 4-4-5 Calendar
    d. Real income

28. _____ is commonly defined as the amount of a company's or a person's income before all deductions or any taxpayer's income, except that which is specifically excluded by the Internal Revenue Code, before taking deductions or taxes into account. For a business, this amount is pre-tax net sales less cost of sales. Section 61 of the Internal Revenue Code (Code) defines '_____' as 'all income from whatever source derived.' Section 61(a) of the Code lists fifteen examples of items included in _____; however, the list is not exhaustive.
    a. Shareholder value
    b. Financial distress
    c. Second lien loan
    d. Gross income

Chapter 3. Sensible Shopping and Spending

1. In economics, business, and accounting, a _____ is the value of money that has been used up to produce something, and hence is not available for use anymore. In business, the _____ may be one of acquisition, in which case the amount of money expended to acquire it is counted as _____. In this case, money is the input that is gone in order to acquire the thing.
   a. Marginal cost
   b. Sliding scale fees
   c. Fixed costs
   d. Cost

2. _____ is buying products in large quantities at a lower price per item than is available for smaller quantities. Wholesale is selling or related to selling goods in large quantities for resale to the consumer. Retailing is buying products in bulk at wholesale, and selling them in small quantities at higher prices.
   a. 7-Eleven
   b. 4-4-5 Calendar
   c. 529 plan
   d. Bulk purchasing

3. The coupon or _____ of a bond is the amount of interest paid per year expressed as a percentage of the face value of the bond.

   For example if you hold $10,000 nominal of a bond described as a 4.5% loan stock, you will receive $450 in interest each year (probably in two installments of $225 each.)

   Not all bonds have coupons.

   a. Revenue bonds
   b. Coupon rate
   c. Zero-coupon bond
   d. Puttable bond

4. An _____ is a retirement plan account that provides some tax advantages for retirement savings in the United States.
   a. ABN Amro
   b. Individual Retirement Arrangement
   c. A Random Walk Down Wall Street
   d. AAB

5. _____ or financing is to provide capital (funds), which means money for a project, a person, a business or any other private or public institutions.

Those funds can be allocated for either short term or long term purposes. The health fund is a new way of _____ private healthcare centers.

   a. Synthetic CDO
   b. Proxy fight
   c. Product life cycle
   d. Funding

6. _____ is the provision of resources (such as granting a loan) by one party to another party where that second party does not reimburse the first party immediately, thereby generating a debt, and instead arranges either to repay or return those resources (or material(s) of equal value) at a later date. The first party is called a creditor, also known as a lender, while the second party is called a debtor, also known as a borrower.

Movements of financial capital are normally dependent on either _____ or equity transfers.

   a. Clearing house
   b. Warrant
   c. Comparable
   d. Credit

7. An _____ is quite usually a standard guarantee from the seller of a product that specifies the extent to which the quality or performance of the product is assured and states the conditions under which the product can be returned, replaced, or repaired. It is often given in the form of a specific, written 'Warranty' document. However, a warranty may also arise by operation of law based upon the seller's description of the goods, and perhaps their source and quality, and any material deviation from that specification would violate the guarantee.
   a. Assumption of risk
   b. Economic depreciation
   c. Economies of scale
   d. Express warranty

8. A '_____' is a 'Charge' that is paid to obtain the right to delay a payment. Essentially, the payer purchases the right to make a given payment in the future instead of in the Present. The '_____', or 'Charge' that must be paid to delay the payment, is simply the difference between what the payment amount would be if it were paid in the present and what the payment amount would be paid if it were paid in the future.

a. Risk aversion
b. Value at risk
c. Discount
d. Risk modeling

9. _____ measures the nominal future sum of money that a given sum of money is 'worth' at a specified time in the future assuming a certain interest rate rate of return; it is the present value multiplied by the accumulation function.

The value does not include corrections for inflation or other factors that affect the true value of money in the future. This is used in time value of money calculations.

a. Future-oriented
b. Present value of costs
c. Discounted cash flow
d. Future value

Chapter 4. Frauds and Swindles and How to Avoid Them

1. In retail sales, a _____ is a form of fraud in which the party putting forth the fraud lures in customers by advertising a product or service at an unprofitably low price, then reveals to potential customers that the advertised good is not available but that a substitute is. This term has lots of other meanings, even outside of the marketing sense.

   The goal of the _____ is to convince some buyers to purchase the substitute good as a means of avoiding disappointment over not getting the bait, or as a way to recover sunk costs expended to try to obtain the bait.

   a. Time value of money
   b. Bait and switch
   c. Zero-coupon bond
   d. Price-to-book ratio

2. A _____ is a plan to acquire high rates of return for a small investment. Most such schemes promise that participants can obtain this high rate of return with little risk.

   Most _____s also promise that little skill, effort, or time is required.

   a. Get-rich-quick scheme
   b. Demand draft
   c. Guinness share-trading fraud
   d. Tobashi scheme

3. An _____ is quite usually a standard guarantee from the seller of a product that specifies the extent to which the quality or performance of the product is assured and states the conditions under which the product can be returned, replaced, or repaired. It is often given in the form of a specific, written 'Warranty' document. However, a warranty may also arise by operation of law based upon the seller's description of the goods, and perhaps their source and quality, and any material deviation from that specification would violate the guarantee.
   a. Economies of scale
   b. Economic depreciation
   c. Assumption of risk
   d. Express warranty

4. A _____ is a fraudulent investment operation that involves paying abnormally high returns to investors out of the money paid in by subsequent investors, rather than from the profit from any real business. It is named after Charles Ponzi. The term '_____' is used primarily in the United States, while other English-speaking countries do not distinguish verbally between this scheme and other forms of pyramid scheme.

Chapter 4. Frauds and Swindles and How to Avoid Them

a. Ponzi scheme
b. 7-Eleven
c. 4-4-5 Calendar
d. 529 plan

5. A _____ is a non-sustainable business model that involves the exchange of money primarily for enrolling other people into the scheme, without any product or service being delivered.

_____s are illegal in many countries, including the United States, the United Kingdom, France, Germany, Canada, Romania, Colombia, Malaysia, Norway, Bulgaria, Australia, New Zealand, Japan, Nepal, Philippines, South Africa, Sri Lanka, Thailand, Iran, and the People's Republic of China. These types of schemes have existed for at least a century.

a. Pyramid scheme
b. 529 plan
c. 4-4-5 Calendar
d. 7-Eleven

6. _____ is the provision of resources (such as granting a loan) by one party to another party where that second party does not reimburse the first party immediately, thereby generating a debt, and instead arranges either to repay or return those resources (or material(s) of equal value) at a later date. The first party is called a creditor, also known as a lender, while the second party is called a debtor, also known as a borrower.

Movements of financial capital are normally dependent on either _____ or equity transfers.

a. Comparable
b. Credit
c. Warrant
d. Clearing house

7. _____ is the value of a homeowner's unencumbered interest in their property, i.e. the difference between the home's fair market value and the unpaid balance of the mortgage and any outstanding debt over the home. _____ increases as the mortgage is paid or as the property enjoys appreciation. This is sometimes called real property value in economics.

a. REIT
b. Liquidation value
c. Real Estate Investment Trust
d. Home equity

Chapter 4. Frauds and Swindles and How to Avoid Them

8. In the United States, the Financial Industry Regulatory Authority (FINRA) is a self-regulatory organization (SRO) under the Securities Exchange Act of 1934, successor to the _____.

FINRA is responsible for regulatory oversight of all securities firms that do business with the public; professional training, testing and licensing of registered persons; arbitration and mediation; market regulation by contract for The NASDAQ Stock Market, Inc., the American Stock Exchange LLC, and the International Securities Exchange, LLC; and industry utilities, such as Trade Reporting Facilities and other over-the-counter operations.

   a. 4-4-5 Calendar
   b. 529 plan
   c. 7-Eleven
   d. NASD

9. In the United States, the Financial Industry Regulatory Authority (FINRA) is a self-regulatory organization (SRO) under the Securities Exchange Act of 1934, successor to the _____, Inc.

FINRA is responsible for regulatory oversight of all securities firms that do business with the public; professional training, testing and licensing of registered persons; arbitration and mediation; market regulation by contract for The NASDAQ Stock Market, Inc., the American Stock Exchange LLC, and the International Securities Exchange, LLC; and industry utilities, such as Trade Reporting Facilities and other over-the-counter operations.

   a. 529 plan
   b. 4-4-5 Calendar
   c. National Association of Securities Dealers
   d. 7-Eleven

10. A _____ is a fungible, negotiable instrument representing financial value. They are broadly categorized into debt securities (such as banknotes, bonds and debentures), and equity securities; e.g., common stocks. The company or other entity issuing the _____ is called the issuer.
   a. Book entry
   b. Securities lending
   c. Security
   d. Tracking stock

11. The U.S. _____ is an independent agency of the United States government which holds primary responsibility for enforcing the federal securities laws and regulating the securities industry, the nation's stock and options exchanges, and other electronic securities markets. The SEC was created by section 4 of the SEC of 1934 (now codified as 15 U.S.C. § 78d and commonly referred to as the 1934 Act.)

a. 4-4-5 Calendar
b. Securities and Exchange Commission
c. 7-Eleven
d. 529 plan

12. In finance, a _____ is a debt security, in which the authorized issuer owes the holders a debt and, depending on the terms of the _____, is obliged to pay interest (the coupon) and/or to repay the principal at a later date, termed maturity.

Thus a _____ is a loan: the issuer is the borrower, the _____ holder is the lender, and the coupon is the interest. _____s provide the borrower with external funds to finance long-term investments, or, in the case of government _____s, to finance current expenditure.

a. Convertible bond
b. Bond
c. Catastrophe bonds
d. Puttable bond

Chapter 5. Transportation: Buying, Financing, and Insuring Your Cars

1. In economics, business, and accounting, a _____ is the value of money that has been used up to produce something, and hence is not available for use anymore. In business, the _____ may be one of acquisition, in which case the amount of money expended to acquire it is counted as _____. In this case, money is the input that is gone in order to acquire the thing.

    a. Fixed costs
    b. Marginal cost
    c. Sliding scale fees
    d. Cost

2. In business, a _____ is the purchase of one company (the target) by another (the acquirer or bidder). In the UK the term refers to the acquisition of a public company whose shares are listed on a stock exchange, in contrast to the acquisition of a private company.

    Before a bidder makes an offer for another company, it usually first informs that company's board of directors.

    a. 529 plan
    b. 4-4-5 Calendar
    c. Stock swap
    d. Takeover

3. The terms _____ , nominal _____ , and effective _____ describe the interest rate for a whole year (annualized), rather than just a monthly fee/rate, as applied on a loan, mortgage, credit card, etc. Those terms have formal, legal definitions in some countries or legal jurisdictions, but in general:

    - The nominal _____ is the simple-interest rate (for a year.)
    - The effective _____ is the fee+compound interest rate (calculated across a year.)

    The nominal _____ is calculated as: the rate, for a payment period, multiplied by the number of payment periods in a year. However, the exact legal definition of 'effective _____' can vary greatly in each jurisdiction, depending on the type of fees included, such as participation fees, loan origination fees, monthly service charges, or late fees. The effective _____ has been called the 'mathematically-true' interest rate for each year. The computation for the effective _____, as the fee+compound interest rate, can also vary depending on whether the up-front fees, such as origination or participation fees, are added to the entire amount, or treated as a short-term loan due in the first payment.

    a. A Random Walk Down Wall Street
    b. AAB
    c. ABN Amro
    d. Annual percentage rate

Chapter 5. Transportation: Buying, Financing, and Insuring Your Cars

4. _____ or financing is to provide capital (funds), which means money for a project, a person, a business or any other private or public institutions.

Those funds can be allocated for either short term or long term purposes. The health fund is a new way of _____ private healthcare centers.

   a. Proxy fight
   b. Synthetic CDO
   c. Funding
   d. Product life cycle

5. _____ is a fee paid on borrowed assets. It is the price paid for the use of borrowed money, or, money earned by deposited funds. Assets that are sometimes lent with _____ include money, shares, consumer goods through hire purchase, major assets such as aircraft, and even entire factories in finance lease arrangements.

   a. Interest
   b. Insolvency
   c. AAB
   d. A Random Walk Down Wall Street

6. An _____ is the price a borrower pays for the use of money they do not own, and the return a lender receives for deferring the use of funds, by lending it to the borrower. _____s are normally expressed as a percentage rate over the period of one year.

_____s targets are also a vital tool of monetary policy and are used to control variables like investment, inflation, and unemployment.

   a. ABN Amro
   b. Interest rate
   c. A Random Walk Down Wall Street
   d. AAB

7. Leasing is a process by which a firm can obtain the use of a certain fixed assets for which it must pay a series of contractual, periodic, tax deductable payments. The lessee is the receiver of the services or the assets under the lease contract and the lessor is the owner of the assets. The relationship between the tenant and the landlord is called a _____, and can be for a fixed or an indefinite period of time (called the term of the lease.)

Chapter 5. Transportation: Buying, Financing, and Insuring Your Cars

   a. Real estate investing
   b. Real Estate Investment Trust
   c. Tenancy
   d. REIT

8. An _____ is a retirement plan account that provides some tax advantages for retirement savings in the United States.
   a. A Random Walk Down Wall Street
   b. ABN Amro
   c. Individual Retirement Arrangement
   d. AAB

9. _____ is a process by which a firm can obtain the use of a certain fixed assets for which it must pay a series of contractual, periodic, tax deductable payments. The lessee is the receiver of the services or the assets under the lease contract and the lessor is the owner of the assets. The relationship between the tenant and the landlord is called a tenancy, and can be for a fixed or an indefinite period of time (called the term of the lease).
   a. Quiet period
   b. Foreign Corrupt Practices Act
   c. Royalties
   d. Leasing

10. An _____ is quite usually a standard guarantee from the seller of a product that specifies the extent to which the quality or performance of the product is assured and states the conditions under which the product can be returned, replaced, or repaired. It is often given in the form of a specific, written 'Warranty' document. However, a warranty may also arise by operation of law based upon the seller's description of the goods, and perhaps their source and quality, and any material deviation from that specification would violate the guarantee.
   a. Economic depreciation
   b. Assumption of risk
   c. Economies of scale
   d. Express warranty

11. In the most general sense, a _____ is anything that is a hindrance, or puts individuals at a disadvantage.

Before we discuss the financial terms, we should note that a _____ can also have a much more important slang meaning.

This is best described in an example.

a. Covenant
b. McFadden Act
c. Limited liability
d. Liability

12. In financial accounting, _____s are precautions for which the amount or probability of occurrence are not known. Typical examples are _____s for warranty costs and _____ for taxes the term reserve is used instead of term _____; such a use, however, is inconsistent with the terminology suggested by International Accounting Standards Board.
a. Petty cash
b. Provision
c. Money measurement concept
d. Momentum Accounting and Triple-Entry Bookkeeping

Chapter 6. Buying a Home

1. _____ refers to a business or organization attempting to acquire goods or services to accomplish the goals of the enterprise. Though there are several organizations that attempt to set standards in the _____ process, processes can vary greatly between organizations. Typically the word '_____' is not used interchangeably with the word 'procurement', since procurement typically includes Expediting, Supplier Quality, and Traffic and Logistics (T'L) in addition to _____.
   a. Purchasing
   b. 529 plan
   c. 4-4-5 Calendar
   d. 7-Eleven

2. _____ or financing is to provide capital (funds), which means money for a project, a person, a business or any other private or public institutions.

   Those funds can be allocated for either short term or long term purposes. The health fund is a new way of _____ private healthcare centers.

   a. Proxy fight
   b. Product life cycle
   c. Synthetic CDO
   d. Funding

3. _____ is the legal and professional proceeding in which a mortgagee usually a lender, obtains a court ordered termination of a mortgagor's equitable right of redemption. Usually a lender obtains a security interest from a borrower who mortgages or pledges an asset like a house to secure the loan. If the borrower defaults and the lender tries to repossess the property, courts of equity can grant the borrower the equitable right of redemption if the borrower repays the debt.
   a. Liability
   b. Federal Acquisition Regulations
   c. Letter of credit
   d. Foreclosure

4. _____s is a real estate appraisal term referring to properties with characteristics that are similar to a subject property whose value is being sought. This can be accomplished either by a real estate agent who attempts to establish the value of a potential client's home or property through market analysis or, by a licensed or certified appraiser or surveyor using more defined methods, when performing a real estate appraisal.

Chapter 6. Buying a Home

Five factors are usually considered when determining _____s:

- Conditions of Sale -- Did the _____ recently transact under conditions (e.g. -- arms length, distress sale, estate settlement) which are consistent with the standard of value under which the appraisal is being performed?
- Financing Conditions -- Was the _____ transaction influenced by non-market or other favorable (or even unfavorable) financing terms? For example, if the _____ sold with a below-market interest rate provided by the seller, and if the standard of value (e.g. -- market value) assumes no such abnormal financing, then the appraiser may need to adjust the _____ price by an amount equal to the estimated impact of the favorable financing.
- Market Conditions -- This is often referred to as the time adjustment and accounts for changing prices over time.
- Locational Comparability -- Are the _____ and the subject property influenced by the same locational characteristics? For example, even two houses in the same neighborhood may have different views which cause one to be more valuable than the other.
- Physical Comparability -- This includes such factors as size, condition, quality, and age.

A real estate appraisal is like any other statistical sampling process. The _____s are the samples drawn and measured, and the outcome is an estimate of value -- called an 'opinion of value' in the terminology of real estate appraisal.

  a. Bucket shop
  b. Procter ' Gamble
  c. Margin
  d. Comparable

5. An _____ is quite usually a standard guarantee from the seller of a product that specifies the extent to which the quality or performance of the product is assured and states the conditions under which the product can be returned, replaced, or repaired. It is often given in the form of a specific, written 'Warranty' document. However, a warranty may also arise by operation of law based upon the seller's description of the goods, and perhaps their source and quality, and any material deviation from that specification would violate the guarantee.
  a. Assumption of risk
  b. Economic depreciation
  c. Express warranty
  d. Economies of scale

6. In economics, business, and accounting, a _____ is the value of money that has been used up to produce something, and hence is not available for use anymore. In business, the _____ may be one of acquisition, in which case the amount of money expended to acquire it is counted as _____. In this case, money is the input that is gone in order to acquire the thing.

a. Cost
b. Sliding scale fees
c. Marginal cost
d. Fixed costs

7. In economics, _____ is a measure of the relative satisfaction from or desirability of consumption of various goods and services. Given this measure, one may speak meaningfully of increasing or decreasing _____, and thereby explain economic behavior in terms of attempts to increase one's _____. For illustrative purposes, changes in _____ are sometimes expressed in units called utils.
    a. AAB
    b. A Random Walk Down Wall Street
    c. Utility function
    d. Utility

8. An _____ is a retirement plan account that provides some tax advantages for retirement savings in the United States.
    a. ABN Amro
    b. A Random Walk Down Wall Street
    c. Individual Retirement Arrangement
    d. AAB

9. A _____ is an exchange of promises between two or more parties to do an act which is enforceable in a court of law. It is where an unqualified offer meets a qualified acceptance and the parties reach Consensus ad Idem. The parties must have the necessary capacity to _____ and the _____ must not be either trifling, indeterminate, impossible or illegal.
    a. Contract
    b. 4-4-5 Calendar
    c. 7-Eleven
    d. 529 plan

10. An _____ is a deposit towards the purchase of real estate or publicly tendered government contract made by a buyer or registered contractor to demonstrate that he/she is serious (earnest) about wanting to complete the purchase. When a buyer makes an offer to buy residential real estate, he/she generally signs a contract and pays a sum acceptable to the seller by way of earnest money. The amount varies enormously, depending upon local custom and the state of the local market at the time of contract negotiations.

a. ABN Amro
b. A Random Walk Down Wall Street
c. Earnest payment
d. AAB

11. An _____ is a non-possessory interest to use real property in possession of another person for a stated purpose. An _____ is considered as a property right in itself at common law and is still treated as a type of property in most jurisdictions. In some jurisdictions, another term for _____ is equitable servitude, although _____s do not have their origin in equity.

a. A Random Walk Down Wall Street
b. ABN Amro
c. AAB
d. Easement

12. In law, a _____ is a form of security interest granted over an item of property to secure the payment of a debt or performance of some other obligation. The owner of the property, who grants the _____, is referred to as the lienor and the person who has the benefit of the _____ is referred to as the _____ee.

The etymological root is: Anglo-French _____, loyen bond, restraint, from Latin ligamen, from ligare to bind.

a. Family and Medical Leave Act
b. Lien
c. Joint venture
d. Sarbanes-Oxley Act

13. A _____, in its most general sense, is a solemn promise to engage in or refrain from a specified action.

More specifically, a _____, in contrast to a contract, is a one-way agreement whereby the _____er is the only party bound by the promise. A _____ may have conditions and prerequisites that qualify the undertaking, including the actions of second or third parties, but there is no inherent agreement by such other parties to fulfill those requirements.

a. Federal Trade Commission Act
b. Clayton Antitrust Act
c. Covenant
d. Partnership

14. _____ in the United States is indemnity insurance against financial loss from defects in title to real property and from the invalidity or unenforceability of mortgage liens. _____ is principally a product developed and sold in the United States as a result of the comparative deficiency of the US land records laws. It is meant to protect an owner's or a lender's financial interest in real property against loss due to title defects, liens or other matters.
   a. Title insurance
   b. Preferred provider organization
   c. 529 plan
   d. 4-4-5 Calendar

15. In finance, _____ occurs when a debtor has not met its legal obligations according to the debt contract, e.g. it has not made a scheduled payment, or has violated a loan covenant (condition) of the debt contract. _____ may occur if the debtor is either unwilling or unable to pay their debt. This can occur with all debt obligations including bonds, mortgages, loans, and promissory notes.
   a. Credit crunch
   b. Debt validation
   c. Default
   d. Vendor finance

16. An _____ account is

   - an account established by a broker, under the provisions of license law, for the purpose of holding funds on behalf of the broker's principal or some other person until the consummation or termination of a transaction, or
   - a trust account held in the borrower's name to pay obligations such as property taxes and insurance premiums.

   _____ is best known in the United States in the context of real estate (specifically in mortgages where the mortgage company establishes an _____ account to pay property tax and insurance during the term of the mortgage.) _____ companies are also commonly used in the transfer of high value personal and business property, like websites and businesses, and in the completion of person-to-person remote auctions (such as eBay.) In the UK _____ accounts are often used during private property transactions to hold solicitors' client's money, such as the deposit, until such time as the transaction completes.

   a. A Random Walk Down Wall Street
   b. ABN Amro
   c. AAB
   d. Escrow

17. The institution most often referenced by the word '_____' is a public or publicly traded _____, the shares of which are traded on a public stock exchange (e.g., the New York Stock Exchange or Nasdaq in the United States) where shares of stock of _____s are bought and sold by and to the general public. Most of the largest businesses in the world are publicly traded _____s. However, the majority of _____s are said to be closely held, privately held or close _____s, meaning that no ready market exists for the trading of shares.

   a. Depository Trust Company
   b. Protect
   c. Federal Home Loan Mortgage Corporation
   d. Corporation

18. The _____, (known as '_____'), was an Act passed by the United States Congress in 1974. It is codified at Title 12, Chapter 27 of the United States Code, 12 U.S.C. Â§ 2601-2617.

The Act prohibits kickbacks between lenders and third-party settlement service agents in the real estate settlement process (Section 8 of _____). Even reciprocal referrals among these types of professions could be construed in court as a violation of the law of _____.

   a. Real Estate Settlement Procedures Act
   b. Fiduciary
   c. Leasing
   d. Federal Trade Commission Act

Chapter 7. Financing a Home

1. _____ or financing is to provide capital (funds), which means money for a project, a person, a business or any other private or public institutions.

   Those funds can be allocated for either short term or long term purposes. The health fund is a new way of _____ private healthcare centers.

   a. Synthetic CDO
   b. Funding
   c. Proxy fight
   d. Product life cycle

2. _____ is the provision of resources (such as granting a loan) by one party to another party where that second party does not reimburse the first party immediately, thereby generating a debt, and instead arranges either to repay or return those resources (or material(s) of equal value) at a later date. The first party is called a creditor, also known as a lender, while the second party is called a debtor, also known as a borrower.

   Movements of financial capital are normally dependent on either _____ or equity transfers.

   a. Credit
   b. Comparable
   c. Warrant
   d. Clearing house

3. _____ is the legal and professional proceeding in which a mortgagee usually a lender, obtains a court ordered termination of a mortgagor's equitable right of redemption. Usually a lender obtains a security interest from a borrower who mortgages or pledges an asset like a house to secure the loan. If the borrower defaults and the lender tries to repossess the property, courts of equity can grant the borrower the equitable right of redemption if the borrower repays the debt.
   a. Liability
   b. Federal Acquisition Regulations
   c. Foreclosure
   d. Letter of credit

4. _____ is a fee paid on borrowed assets. It is the price paid for the use of borrowed money , or, money earned by deposited funds . Assets that are sometimes lent with _____ include money, shares, consumer goods through hire purchase, major assets such as aircraft, and even entire factories in finance lease arrangements.
   a. A Random Walk Down Wall Street
   b. Insolvency
   c. AAB
   d. Interest

Chapter 7. Financing a Home 31

5. An _____ is the price a borrower pays for the use of money they do not own, and the return a lender receives for deferring the use of funds, by lending it to the borrower. _____s are normally expressed as a percentage rate over the period of one year.

_____s targets are also a vital tool of monetary policy and are used to control variables like investment, inflation, and unemployment.

   a. A Random Walk Down Wall Street
   b. Interest rate
   c. ABN Amro
   d. AAB

6. The terms _____ , nominal _____, and effective _____ describe the interest rate for a whole year (annualized), rather than just a monthly fee/rate, as applied on a loan, mortgage, credit card, etc. Those terms have formal, legal definitions in some countries or legal jurisdictions, but in general:

- The nominal _____ is the simple-interest rate (for a year.)
- The effective _____ is the fee+compound interest rate (calculated across a year.)

The nominal _____ is calculated as: the rate, for a payment period, multiplied by the number of payment periods in a year. However, the exact legal definition of 'effective _____' can vary greatly in each jurisdiction, depending on the type of fees included, such as participation fees, loan origination fees, monthly service charges, or late fees. The effective _____ has been called the 'mathematically-true' interest rate for each year. The computation for the effective _____, as the fee+compound interest rate, can also vary depending on whether the up-front fees, such as origination or participation fees, are added to the entire amount, or treated as a short-term loan due in the first payment.

   a. A Random Walk Down Wall Street
   b. ABN Amro
   c. AAB
   d. Annual percentage rate

Chapter 7. Financing a Home

7. _____ is the process of decreasing an amount over a period of time. The word comes from Middle English amortisen to kill, alienate in mortmain, from Anglo-French amorteser, alteration of amortir, from Vulgar Latin admortire to kill, from Latin ad- + mort-, mors death. Particular instances of the term include:

- _____ (business), the allocation of a lump sum amount to different time periods, particularly for loans and other forms of finance, including related interest or other finance charges.
  - _____ schedule, a table detailing each periodic payment on a loan (typically a mortgage), as generated by an _____ calculator.
  - Negative _____, an _____ schedule where the loan amount actually increases through not paying the full interest
- Amortized analysis, analyzing the execution cost of algorithms over a sequence of operations.
- _____ of capital expenditures of certain assets under accounting rules, particularly intangible assets, in a manner analogous to depreciation.
- _____ (tax law)

_____ is also used in the context of zoning regulations and describes the time in which a property owner has to relocate when the property's use constitutes a preexisting nonconforming use under zoning regulations.

- Depreciation

a. Option
b. Amortization
c. AT'T Inc.
d. Intrinsic value

8. In finance, a _____ is collateral that the holder of a position in securities, options, or futures contracts has to deposit to cover the credit risk of his counterparty (most often his broker.) This risk can arise if the holder has done any of the following:

- borrowed cash from the counterparty to buy securities or options,
- sold securities or options short, or
- entered into a futures contract.

The collateral can be in the form of cash or securities, and it is deposited in a _____ account. On U.S. futures exchanges, '_____' was formally called performance bond.

_____ buying is buying securities with cash borrowed from a broker, using other securities as collateral.

a. Share
b. Margin
c. Credit
d. Procter ' Gamble

9. _____ is buying securities with cash borrowed from a broker, using other securities as collateral. This has the effect of magnifying any profit or loss made on the securities. The securities serve as collateral for the loan.

a. Risk-neutral measure
b. Triple witching hour
c. SPI 200 futures contract
d. Margin buying

10. The phrase _____ refers to the aspect of corporate strategy, corporate finance and management dealing with the buying, selling and combining of different companies that can aid, finance, or help a growing company in a given industry grow rapidly without having to create another business entity.

An acquisition, also known as a takeover, is the buying of one company (the 'target') by another. An acquisition may be friendly or hostile.

a. 529 plan
b. 4-4-5 Calendar
c. 7-Eleven
d. Mergers and acquisitions

11. _____ is insurance payable to a lender or trustee for a pool of securities that may be required when taking out a mortgage loan. It is insurance to offset losses in the case where a mortgagor is not able to repay the loan and the lender is not able to recover its costs after foreclosure and sale of the mortgaged property. Typical rates are $55/mo. per $100,000 financed, or as high as $1,500/yr. for a typical $200,000 loan.

a. Property insurance
b. 529 plan
c. 4-4-5 Calendar
d. Lenders Mortgage Insurance

12. In economics, business, and accounting, a _____ is the value of money that has been used up to produce something, and hence is not available for use anymore. In business, the _____ may be one of acquisition, in which case the amount of money expended to acquire it is counted as _____. In this case, money is the input that is gone in order to acquire the thing.

a. Sliding scale fees
b. Fixed costs
c. Marginal cost
d. Cost

13. _____ is an insurance policy which compensates lenders or investors for losses due to the default of a mortgage loan. _____ can be either public or private depending upon the insurer. The policy is also known as a mortgage indemnity guarantee (Mortgage insuranceG), particularly in the UK.

a. Reverse mortgage
b. Subprime lending
c. Mortgage-backed security
d. Mortgage insurance

14. An _____ account is

- an account established by a broker, under the provisions of license law, for the purpose of holding funds on behalf of the broker's principal or some other person until the consummation or termination of a transaction, or
- a trust account held in the borrower's name to pay obligations such as property taxes and insurance premiums.

_____ is best known in the United States in the context of real estate (specifically in mortgages where the mortgage company establishes an _____ account to pay property tax and insurance during the term of the mortgage.) _____ companies are also commonly used in the transfer of high value personal and business property, like websites and businesses, and in the completion of person-to-person remote auctions (such as eBay.) In the UK _____ accounts are often used during private property transactions to hold solicitors' client's money, such as the deposit, until such time as the transaction completes.

a. Escrow
b. A Random Walk Down Wall Street
c. ABN Amro
d. AAB

15. In financial accounting, the term _____ is most commonly used to describe any part of shareholders' equity, except for basic share capital. Sometimes, the term is used instead of the term provision; such a use, however, is inconsistent with the terminology suggested by International Accounting Standards Board. For more information about provisions, see provision (accounting.)

a. Treasury stock
b. Closing entries
c. Reserve
d. FIFO and LIFO accounting

16. _____, in bookkeeping, refers to assets, liabilities, income, and expenses recorded on individual pages of the so called book of final entry or ledger. Changes in _____ value are made by chronologically posting debit (DR) and credit (CR) entries to its page. Examples of _____s are cash, _____s receivable, mortgages, loans, land and buildings, common stock, sales, services provided, wages, and payroll overhead.
a. Accretion
b. Option
c. Alpha
d. Account

17. _____ is early repayment of a loan by a borrower.

In the case of a mortgage-backed security (MBS), _____ is perceived as a risk, because mortgage debts are often paid off early in order to incur lower total interest payments through cheaper refinancing. The new financing may be cheaper because the borrower's credit rating has improved or because interest rates are lower, but in either case, the payments that would have been made to the MBS investor would be above market rates.

a. Prepayment
b. Disposal tax effect
c. Bankruptcy remote
d. Retention ratio

18. The institution most often referenced by the word '_____' is a public or publicly traded _____, the shares of which are traded on a public stock exchange (e.g., the New York Stock Exchange or Nasdaq in the United States) where shares of stock of _____s are bought and sold by and to the general public. Most of the largest businesses in the world are publicly traded _____s. However, the majority of _____s are said to be closely held, privately held or close _____s, meaning that no ready market exists for the trading of shares.
a. Depository Trust Company
b. Federal Home Loan Mortgage Corporation
c. Corporation
d. Protect

Chapter 7. Financing a Home

19. The _____ (NYSE: FNM), commonly known as Fannie Mae, is a stockholder-owned corporation chartered by Congress in 1968 as a government sponsored enterprise (GSE), but founded in 1938 during the Great Depression. The corporation's purpose is to purchase and securitize mortgages in order to ensure that funds are consistently available to the institutions that lend money to home buyers.

On September 7, 2008, James Lockhart, director of the Federal Housing Finance Agency (FHFA), announced that Fannie Mae and Freddie Mac were being placed into conservatorship of the FHFA.

   a. SPDR
   b. Federal National Mortgage Association
   c. The Depository Trust ' Clearing Corporation
   d. General partnership

20. The _____ (NYSE: FRE) is an insolvent government sponsored enterprise (GSE) of the United States federal government.

The _____ was created in 1970 to expand the secondary market for mortgages in the US. Along with other GSEs, Freddie Mac buys mortgages on the secondary market, pools them, and sells them as mortgage-backed securities to investors on the open market.

   a. Governmental Accounting Standards Board
   b. The Depository Trust ' Clearing Corporation
   c. Federal Home Loan Mortgage Corporation
   d. Public company

21. The _____ is a U.S. government-owned corporation within the Department of Housing and Urban Development

Ginnie Mae provides guarantees on mortgage-backed securities backed by federally insured or guaranteed loans, mainly loans issued by the Federal Housing Administration, Department of Veterans Affairs, Rural Housing Service, and Office of Public and Indian Housing. Ginnie Mae securities are the only MBS that are guaranteed by the United States government.

   a. Certified Emission Reductions
   b. GNMA
   c. Case-Shiller Home Price Indices
   d. Cash budget

Chapter 7. Financing a Home

22. A _____ is a bond issued by a national government denominated in the country's own currency. Bonds issued by national governments in foreign currencies are normally referred to as sovereign bonds. The first ever _____ was issued by the British government in 1693 to raise money to fund a war against France.

   a. Zero-coupon bond
   b. Government bond
   c. Collateralized debt obligations
   d. Municipal bond

23. In finance, a _____ is a debt security, in which the authorized issuer owes the holders a debt and, depending on the terms of the _____, is obliged to pay interest (the coupon) and/or to repay the principal at a later date, termed maturity.

   Thus a _____ is a loan: the issuer is the borrower, the _____ holder is the lender, and the coupon is the interest. _____s provide the borrower with external funds to finance long-term investments, or, in the case of government _____s, to finance current expenditure.

   a. Puttable bond
   b. Catastrophe bonds
   c. Bond
   d. Convertible bond

24. _____ is a term used in the context of the purchase of expensive items such as a car and a house, whereby the payment is the initial upfront portion of the total amount due and it is usually given in cash at the time of finalizing the transaction. A loan is then required to make the full payment.

   The main purpose of a _____ is to ensure that the lending institution can recover the balance due on the loan in the event that the borrower defaults.

   a. Business valuation
   b. Financial Institutions Reform Recovery and Enforcement Act
   c. Down payment
   d. Royalties

25. In the United States, a _____ is a mortgage with a loan amount above the industry-standard definition of conventional conforming loan limits. This standard is set by the two largest secondary market lenders, Fannie Mae and Freddie Mac. Loans above the conforming limits may be offered by seller servicers of these wholesale institutions, as well as Wall Street conduits who provide warehouse financing for mortgage lenders.

a. Graduated payment mortgage
b. 4-4-5 Calendar
c. Government National Mortgage Association
d. Jumbo mortgage

26. The _____, (known as '_____'), was an Act passed by the United States Congress in 1974. It is codified at Title 12, Chapter 27 of the United States Code, 12 U.S.C. Â§ 2601-2617.

The Act prohibits kickbacks between lenders and third-party settlement service agents in the real estate settlement process (Section 8 of _____). Even reciprocal referrals among these types of professions could be construed in court as a violation of the law of _____.

a. Federal Trade Commission Act
b. Leasing
c. Fiduciary
d. Real Estate Settlement Procedures Act

27. A _____ is an exchange of promises between two or more parties to do an act which is enforceable in a court of law. It is where an unqualified offer meets a qualified acceptance and the parties reach Consensus ad Idem. The parties must have the necessary capacity to _____ and the _____ must not be either trifling, indeterminate, impossible or illegal.
a. 529 plan
b. 7-Eleven
c. 4-4-5 Calendar
d. Contract

28. _____ is a term used in accounting relating to the increase in value of an asset. In this sense it is the reverse of depreciation, which measures the fall in value of assets over their normal life-time.

_____ is a rise of a currency in a floating exchange rate.

a. Appreciation
b. Other Comprehensive Basis of Accounting
c. Operating cash flow
d. A Random Walk Down Wall Street

Chapter 8. Housing Costs and Regulations

1. _____ is a term used in accounting relating to the increase in value of an asset. In this sense it is the reverse of depreciation, which measures the fall in value of assets over their normal life-time.

   _____ is a rise of a currency in a floating exchange rate.

   a. Appreciation
   b. Other Comprehensive Basis of Accounting
   c. A Random Walk Down Wall Street
   d. Operating cash flow

2. _____ is a term used in accounting, economics and finance to spread the cost of an asset over the span of several years.

   In simple words we can say that _____ is the reduction in the value of an asset due to usage, passage of time, wear and tear, technological outdating or obsolescence, depletion or other such factors.

   In accounting, _____ is a term used to describe any method of attributing the historical or purchase cost of an asset across its useful life, roughly corresponding to normal wear and tear.

   a. Bottom line
   b. Deferred financing costs
   c. Matching principle
   d. Depreciation

3. _____ provides protection against most risks to property, such as fire, theft and some weather damage. This includes specialized forms of insurance such as fire insurance, flood insurance, earthquake insurance, home insurance or boiler insurance. Property is insured in two main ways - open perils and named perils.
   a. Lenders Mortgage Insurance
   b. Property insurance
   c. 529 plan
   d. 4-4-5 Calendar

4. In the most general sense, a _____ is anything that is a hindrance, or puts individuals at a disadvantage.

   Before we discuss the financial terms, we should note that a _____ can also have a much more important slang meaning.

   This is best described in an example.

Chapter 8. Housing Costs and Regulations

a. Limited liability
b. Liability
c. Covenant
d. McFadden Act

5. _____ is a type of property. In the common law systems _____ may also be called chattels or personalty. It is distinguished from real property, or real estate.
   a. Personal property
   b. Beneficial owner
   c. Loan agreement
   d. McFadden Act

6. _____ is an insurance-related term that describes a splitting or spreading of risk among multiple parties.

In the US insurance market, _____ is the joint assumption of risk between the insurer and the insured. In title insurance it also means the sharing of risks between two or more title insurance companies.

   a. 7-Eleven
   b. 4-4-5 Calendar
   c. 529 plan
   d. Coinsurance

7. In economics, business, and accounting, a _____ is the value of money that has been used up to produce something, and hence is not available for use anymore. In business, the _____ may be one of acquisition, in which case the amount of money expended to acquire it is counted as _____. In this case, money is the input that is gone in order to acquire the thing.
   a. Marginal cost
   b. Cost
   c. Sliding scale fees
   d. Fixed costs

8. An _____ is a retirement plan account that provides some tax advantages for retirement savings in the United States.

a. AAB
b. Individual Retirement Arrangement
c. ABN Amro
d. A Random Walk Down Wall Street

9. An _____ is an inspection, survey and analysis of energy flows in a building, process or system with the objective of understanding the energy dynamics of the system under study. Typically an _____ is conducted to seek opportunities to reduce the amount of energy input into the system without negatively affecting the output(s.) When the object of study is an occupied building then reducing energy consumption while maintaining or improving human comfort, health and safety are of primary concern.
   a. A Random Walk Down Wall Street
   b. AAB
   c. ABN Amro
   d. Energy audit

10. In economics, _____ is a measure of the relative satisfaction from or desirability of consumption of various goods and services. Given this measure, one may speak meaningfully of increasing or decreasing _____, and thereby explain economic behavior in terms of attempts to increase one's _____. For illustrative purposes, changes in _____ are sometimes expressed in units called utils.
    a. AAB
    b. A Random Walk Down Wall Street
    c. Utility function
    d. Utility

11. _____, compulsory purchase (United Kingdom, New Zealand, Ireland), resumption/compulsory acquisition (Australia) or expropriation (South Africa and Canada) or land acqusition (India) in common law legal systems is the inherent power of the state to seize a citizen's private property, expropriate property, or seize a citizens rights in property with due monetary compensation, but without the owner's consent. The property is taken either for government use or by delegation to third parties who will devote it to public or civic use or, in some cases, economic development. The most common uses of property taken by _____ are for public utilities, highways, and railroads.
    a. ABN Amro
    b. AAB
    c. Eminent domain
    d. A Random Walk Down Wall Street

12. _____ refers to laws or ordinances that set price controls on the renting of residential housing. It functions as a price ceiling.

Chapter 8. Housing Costs and Regulations

_____ exists in approximately 40 countries around the world.

a. 4-4-5 Calendar
b. Rent control
c. 529 plan
d. 7-Eleven

13. _____ is an insurance policy which compensates lenders or investors for losses due to the default of a mortgage loan. _____ can be either public or private depending upon the insurer. The policy is also known as a mortgage indemnity guarantee (Mortgage insuranceG), particularly in the UK.

a. Subprime lending
b. Mortgage-backed security
c. Mortgage insurance
d. Reverse mortgage

14. _____ is a list for goods and materials held available in stock by a business. It is also used for a list of the contents of a household and for a list for testamentary purposes of the possessions of someone who has died. In accounting _____ is considered an asset.

a. AAB
b. A Random Walk Down Wall Street
c. ABN Amro
d. Inventory

Chapter 9. Renting

1. An _____ is a retirement plan account that provides some tax advantages for retirement savings in the United States.
   a. Individual Retirement Arrangement
   b. A Random Walk Down Wall Street
   c. ABN Amro
   d. AAB

2. In economics, _____ is a rise in the general level of prices of goods and services in an economy over a period of time. The term '_____' once referred to increases in the money supply (monetary _____); however, economic debates about the relationship between money supply and price levels have led to its primary use today in describing price _____. _____ can also be described as a decline in the real value of money--a loss of purchasing power in the medium of exchange which is also the monetary unit of account.
   a. Inflation
   b. AAB
   c. A Random Walk Down Wall Street
   d. ABN Amro

3. In economics, business, and accounting, a _____ is the value of money that has been used up to produce something, and hence is not available for use anymore. In business, the _____ may be one of acquisition, in which case the amount of money expended to acquire it is counted as _____. In this case, money is the input that is gone in order to acquire the thing.
   a. Fixed costs
   b. Sliding scale fees
   c. Marginal cost
   d. Cost

4. In financial accounting, _____s are precautions for which the amount or probability of occurrence are not known. Typical examples are _____s for warranty costs and _____ for taxes the term reserve is used instead of term _____; such a use, however, is inconsistent with the terminology suggested by International Accounting Standards Board.
   a. Momentum Accounting and Triple-Entry Bookkeeping
   b. Money measurement concept
   c. Petty cash
   d. Provision

5. _____ or financing is to provide capital (funds), which means money for a project, a person, a business or any other private or public institutions.

Those funds can be allocated for either short term or long term purposes. The health fund is a new way of _____ private healthcare centers.

a. Synthetic CDO
b. Proxy fight
c. Product life cycle
d. Funding

6. Leasing is a process by which a firm can obtain the use of a certain fixed assets for which it must pay a series of contractual, periodic, tax deductable payments. The lessee is the receiver of the services or the assets under the lease contract and the lessor is the owner of the assets. The relationship between the tenant and the landlord is called a _____, and can be for a fixed or an indefinite period of time (called the term of the lease.)

a. Real estate investing
b. Real Estate Investment Trust
c. Tenancy
d. REIT

7. A _____ is a fungible, negotiable instrument representing financial value. They are broadly categorized into debt securities (such as banknotes, bonds and debentures), and equity securities; e.g., common stocks. The company or other entity issuing the _____ is called the issuer.

a. Tracking stock
b. Book entry
c. Security
d. Securities lending

8. _____ is a process by which a firm can obtain the use of a certain fixed assets for which it must pay a series of contractual, periodic, tax deductable payments. The lessee is the receiver of the services or the assets under the lease contract and the lessor is the owner of the assets. The relationship between the tenant and the landlord is called a tenancy, and can be for a fixed or an indefinite period of time (called the term of the lease).

a. Foreign Corrupt Practices Act
b. Royalties
c. Quiet period
d. Leasing

Chapter 9. Renting

9. An _____ is a contract written by a seller that conveys to the buyer the right -- but not the obligation -- to buy (in the case of a call _____) or to sell (in the case of a put _____) a particular asset, such as a piece of property such as, among others, a futures contract. In return for granting the _____, the seller collects a payment (the premium) from the buyer.

For example, buying a call _____ provides the right to buy a specified quantity of a security at a set strike price at some time on or before expiration, while buying a put _____ provides the right to sell.

   a. Option
   b. Amortization
   c. AT'T Mobility LLC
   d. Annuity

10. In finance, a _____ is a debt security, in which the authorized issuer owes the holders a debt and, depending on the terms of the _____, is obliged to pay interest (the coupon) and/or to repay the principal at a later date, termed maturity.

Thus a _____ is a loan: the issuer is the borrower, the _____ holder is the lender, and the coupon is the interest. _____s provide the borrower with external funds to finance long-term investments, or, in the case of government _____s, to finance current expenditure.

   a. Puttable bond
   b. Catastrophe bonds
   c. Bond
   d. Convertible bond

11. _____ is a contractual right that gives its holder the option to enter a business transaction with the owner of something, according to specified terms, before the owner is entitled to enter into that transaction with a third party. In brief, the _____ is similar in concept to a call option.

An _____ can cover almost any sort of asset, including real estate, personal property, a patent license, a screenplay, or an interest in a business.

   a. 7-Eleven
   b. 529 plan
   c. 4-4-5 Calendar
   d. Right of first refusal

12. _____ refers to laws or ordinances that set price controls on the renting of residential housing. It functions as a price ceiling.

_____ exists in approximately 40 countries around the world.

   a. 4-4-5 Calendar
   b. 7-Eleven
   c. 529 plan
   d. Rent control

Chapter 10. Selling Your Home

1. _____s is a real estate appraisal term referring to properties with characteristics that are similar to a subject property whose value is being sought. This can be accomplished either by a real estate agent who attempts to establish the value of a potential client's home or property through market analysis or, by a licensed or certified appraiser or surveyor using more defined methods, when performing a real estate appraisal.

Five factors are usually considered when determining _____s:

- Conditions of Sale -- Did the _____ recently transact under conditions (e.g. -- arms length, distress sale, estate settlement) which are consistent with the standard of value under which the appraisal is being performed?
- Financing Conditions -- Was the _____ transaction influenced by non-market or other favorable (or even unfavorable) financing terms? For example, if the _____ sold with a below-market interest rate provided by the seller, and if the standard of value (e.g. -- market value) assumes no such abnormal financing, then the appraiser may need to adjust the _____ price by an amount equal to the estimated impact of the favorable financing.
- Market Conditions -- This is often referred to as the time adjustment and accounts for changing prices over time.
- Locational Comparability -- Are the _____ and the subject property influenced by the same locational characteristics? For example, even two houses in the same neighborhood may have different views which cause one to be more valuable than the other.
- Physical Comparability -- This includes such factors as size, condition, quality, and age.

A real estate appraisal is like any other statistical sampling process. The _____s are the samples drawn and measured, and the outcome is an estimate of value -- called an 'opinion of value' in the terminology of real estate appraisal.

a. Margin
b. Procter ' Gamble
c. Bucket shop
d. Comparable

2. _____ or financing is to provide capital (funds), which means money for a project, a person, a business or any other private or public institutions.

Those funds can be allocated for either short term or long term purposes. The health fund is a new way of _____ private healthcare centers.

a. Product life cycle
b. Funding
c. Proxy fight
d. Synthetic CDO

Chapter 10. Selling Your Home

3. _____ refers to the replacement of an existing debt obligation with a debt obligation bearing different terms. The most common consumer _____ is for a home mortgage.

_____ may be undertaken to reduce interest rate/interest costs (by _____ at a lower rate), to extend the repayment time, to pay off other debt(s), to reduce one's periodic payment obligations (sometimes by taking a longer-term loan), to reduce or alter risk (such as by _____ from a variable-rate to a fixed-rate loan), and/or to raise cash for investment, consumption, or the payment of a dividend.

   a. 4-4-5 Calendar
   b. 7-Eleven
   c. 529 plan
   d. Refinancing

4. _____ refers to a business or organization attempting to acquire goods or services to accomplish the goals of the enterprise. Though there are several organizations that attempt to set standards in the _____ process, processes can vary greatly between organizations. Typically the word '_____' is not used interchangeably with the word 'procurement', since procurement typically includes Expediting, Supplier Quality, and Traffic and Logistics (T'L) in addition to _____.
   a. Purchasing
   b. 529 plan
   c. 4-4-5 Calendar
   d. 7-Eleven

5. A _____ is an exchange of promises between two or more parties to do an act which is enforceable in a court of law. It is where an unqualified offer meets a qualified acceptance and the parties reach Consensus ad Idem. The parties must have the necessary capacity to _____ and the _____ must not be either trifling, indeterminate, impossible or illegal.
   a. 7-Eleven
   b. 529 plan
   c. 4-4-5 Calendar
   d. Contract

6. An _____ is a retirement plan account that provides some tax advantages for retirement savings in the United States.
   a. A Random Walk Down Wall Street
   b. ABN Amro
   c. Individual Retirement Arrangement
   d. AAB

7. In economics, business, and accounting, a _____ is the value of money that has been used up to produce something, and hence is not available for use anymore. In business, the _____ may be one of acquisition, in which case the amount of money expended to acquire it is counted as _____. In this case, money is the input that is gone in order to acquire the thing.
   a. Sliding scale fees
   b. Marginal cost
   c. Cost
   d. Fixed costs

Chapter 11. Financial Institutions

1. A _____ is a type of financial intermediary and a type of bank. Commercial banking is also known as business banking. It is a bank that provides checking accounts, savings accounts, and money market accounts and that accepts time deposits.

    a. Commercial bank
    b. 4-4-5 Calendar
    c. 529 plan
    d. 7-Eleven

2. The institution most often referenced by the word '_____' is a public or publicly traded _____, the shares of which are traded on a public stock exchange (e.g., the New York Stock Exchange or Nasdaq in the United States) where shares of stock of _____s are bought and sold by and to the general public. Most of the largest businesses in the world are publicly traded _____s. However, the majority of _____s are said to be closely held, privately held or close _____s, meaning that no ready market exists for the trading of shares.

    a. Protect
    b. Depository Trust Company
    c. Corporation
    d. Federal Home Loan Mortgage Corporation

3. Explicit _____ is a measure implemented in many countries to protect bank depositors, in full or in part, from losses caused by a bank's inability to pay its debts when due. _____ systems are one component of a financial system safety net that promotes financial stability.

    a. Reserve requirement
    b. Deposit Insurance
    c. Time deposit
    d. Banking panic

4. The _____ is a United States government corporation created by the Glass-Steagall Act of 1933. It provides deposit insurance, which guarantees the safety of checking and savings deposits in member banks, currently up to $250,000 per depositor per bank. Insured deposits are backed by the full faith and credit of the United States.

    a. FASB
    b. Ford Foundation
    c. NYSE Group
    d. Federal Deposit Insurance Corporation

Chapter 11. Financial Institutions

5. _____ is the provision of resources (such as granting a loan) by one party to another party where that second party does not reimburse the first party immediately, thereby generating a debt, and instead arranges either to repay or return those resources (or material(s) of equal value) at a later date. The first party is called a creditor, also known as a lender, while the second party is called a debtor, also known as a borrower.

Movements of financial capital are normally dependent on either _____ or equity transfers.

   a. Clearing house
   b. Warrant
   c. Comparable
   d. Credit

6. A _____ is a cooperative financial institution that is owned and controlled by its members, and operated for the purpose of promoting thrift, providing credit at reasonable rates, and providing other financial services to its members. Many _____s exist to further community development or sustainable international development on a local level. Worldwide, _____ systems vary significantly in terms of total system assets and average institution asset size since _____s exist in a wide range of sizes, ranging from volunteer operations with a handful of members to institutions with several billion dollars in assets and hundreds of thousands of members.
   a. Credit Union Service Organization
   b. Fi-linx
   c. Corporate credit union
   d. Credit union

7. A _____ is a financial institution that specializes in accepting savings deposits and making mortgage and other loans. The S'L or thrift term is mainly used in the United States; similar institutions in the United Kingdom, Ireland and some Commonwealth countries include building societies and trustee savings banks.

They are often mutually held, meaning that the depositors and borrowers are members with voting rights, and have the ability to direct the financial and managerial goals of the organization, not unlike the poliyholders of a mutual insurance company.

   a. Net asset value
   b. Mutual fund
   c. Person-to-person lending
   d. Savings and loan association

8. A _____ is a small, short-term loan that is intended to cover a borrower's expenses until his or her next payday. The loans are also sometimes referred to as cash advances, though that term can also refer to cash provided against a prearranged line of credit such as a credit card Legislation regarding _____s varies widely between different countries and, within the USA, between different states.

Chapter 11. Financial Institutions

   a. Payday loan
   b. 529 plan
   c. 4-4-5 Calendar
   d. 7-Eleven

9. _____ is the task of determining how a business will afford to achieve its strategic goals and objectives. Usually, a company creates a Financial Plan immediately after the vision and objectives have been set. The Financial Plan describes each of the activities, resources, equipment and materials that are needed to achieve these objectives, as well as the timeframes involved.
   a. Management by exception
   b. Performance measurement
   c. Financial Planning
   d. Corporate Transparency

10. _____, in bookkeeping, refers to assets, liabilities, income, and expenses recorded on individual pages of the so called book of final entry or ledger. Changes in _____ value are made by chronologically posting debit (DR) and credit (CR) entries to its page. Examples of _____s are cash, _____s receivable, mortgages, loans, land and buildings, common stock, sales, services provided, wages, and payroll overhead.
   a. Option
   b. Alpha
   c. Account
   d. Accretion

11. _____ of a financial instrument such as a check is only a signature, not indicating the payee. The effect of this is that it is payable only to the bearer.

It is 'an endorsement consisting of nothing but a signature and allowing any party in possession of the endorsed item to execute a claim.'

A _____ is commonly known and accepted in the legal and business worlds.

   a. Cramdown
   b. Day trading
   c. Blank endorsement
   d. Consumer debt

12. An account statement or a _____ is a summary of all financial transactions occurring over a given period of time on a deposit account, a credit card, or any other type of account offered by a financial institution.

Chapter 11. Financial Institutions

_____s are typically printed on one or several pieces of paper and either mailed directly to the account holder's address, or kept at the financial institution's local branch for pick-up. Certain ATMs offer the possibility to print, at any time, a condensed version of a _____.

   a. Deposit account
   b. Bilateral netting
   c. 4-4-5 Calendar
   d. Bank statement

13. _____ is a fee paid on borrowed assets. It is the price paid for the use of borrowed money , or, money earned by deposited funds . Assets that are sometimes lent with _____ include money, shares, consumer goods through hire purchase, major assets such as aircraft, and even entire factories in finance lease arrangements.
   a. A Random Walk Down Wall Street
   b. AAB
   c. Interest
   d. Insolvency

14. An _____ is the price a borrower pays for the use of money they do not own, and the return a lender receives for deferring the use of funds, by lending it to the borrower. _____s are normally expressed as a percentage rate over the period of one year.

_____s targets are also a vital tool of monetary policy and are used to control variables like investment, inflation, and unemployment.

   a. ABN Amro
   b. Interest rate
   c. A Random Walk Down Wall Street
   d. AAB

15. The terms _____ , nominal _____, and effective _____ describe the interest rate for a whole year (annualized), rather than just a monthly fee/rate, as applied on a loan, mortgage, credit card, etc. Those terms have formal, legal definitions in some countries or legal jurisdictions, but in general:

   - The nominal _____ is the simple-interest rate (for a year.)
   - The effective _____ is the fee+compound interest rate (calculated across a year.)

The nominal _____ is calculated as: the rate, for a payment period, multiplied by the number of payment periods in a year. However, the exact legal definition of 'effective _____' can vary greatly in each jurisdiction, depending on the type of fees included, such as participation fees, loan origination fees, monthly service charges, or late fees. The effective _____ has been called the 'mathematically-true' interest rate for each year. The computation for the effective _____, as the fee+compound interest rate, can also vary depending on whether the up-front fees, such as origination or participation fees, are added to the entire amount, or treated as a short-term loan due in the first payment.

    a. AAB
    b. A Random Walk Down Wall Street
    c. ABN Amro
    d. Annual percentage rate

16. A _____ s a time deposit, a financial product commonly offered to consumers by banks, thrift institutions, and credit unions.

They are similar to savings accounts in that they are insured and thus virtually risk-free; they are 'money in the bank'. They are different from savings accounts in that they have a specific, fixed term (often three months, six months, or one to five years), and, usually, a fixed interest rate.

    a. Time deposit
    b. Reserve requirement
    c. Variable rate mortgage
    d. Certificate of deposit

17. In finance, the _____ is the global financial market for short-term borrowing and lending. It provides short-term liquidity funding for the global financial system. The _____ is where short-term obligations such as Treasury bills, commercial paper and bankers' acceptances are bought and sold.
    a. Debt-for-equity swap
    b. Money market
    c. Cramdown
    d. Consumer debt

18. _____ is that which is owed; usually referencing assets owed, but the term can cover other obligations. In the case of assets, _____ is a means of using future purchasing power in the present before a summation has been earned. Some companies and corporations use _____ as a part of their overall corporate finance strategy.

a. Partial Payment
b. Credit cycle
c. Cross-collateralization
d. Debt

19. _____ broadly refers to regulation of the debt collection industry at both the U.S. Federal and state levels of government. At the Federal level, it is primarily governed by the _____ Practices Act ('_____PA'.) In addition, many U.S. States also have debt collection laws that regulate the credit and collection industry and give consumer debtors protection from abusive and deceptive practices.
   a. Covenant
   b. Securities Investor Protection Act
   c. Bundesrechnungshof
   d. Fair Debt Collection

20. A _____, referred to as a note payable in accounting, is a contract where one party (the maker or issuer) makes an unconditional promise in writing to pay a sum of money to the other (the payee), either at a fixed or determinable future time or on demand of the payee, under specific terms. They differ from IOUs in that they contain a specific promise to pay, rather than simply acknowledging that a debt exists.

The terms of a note typically include the principal amount, the interest rate if any, and the maturity date.

   a. Promissory note
   b. Title loan
   c. Financial plan
   d. Credit repair software

21. _____ expresses an annual rate of interest taking into account the effect of compounding, usually for deposit or investment products (such as a certificate of deposit.) It is analogous to the Annual percentage rate (APR), which is used for loans. In some jurisdictions, the use and definition of _____ may be regulated by a government agency, in which case it would generally be capitalized.
   a. AAB
   b. ABN Amro
   c. A Random Walk Down Wall Street
   d. Annual Percentage Yield

22. In finance, the term _____ describes the amount in cash that returns to the owners of a security. Normally it does not include the price variations, at the difference of the total return. _____ applies to various stated rates of return on stocks (common and preferred, and convertible), fixed income instruments (bonds, notes, bills, strips, zero coupon), and some other investment type insurance products (e.g. annuities.)
   a. Yield to maturity
   b. Macaulay duration
   c. 4-4-5 Calendar
   d. Yield

23. In economics, business, and accounting, a _____ is the value of money that has been used up to produce something, and hence is not available for use anymore. In business, the _____ may be one of acquisition, in which case the amount of money expended to acquire it is counted as _____. In this case, money is the input that is gone in order to acquire the thing.
   a. Fixed costs
   b. Marginal cost
   c. Cost
   d. Sliding scale fees

Chapter 12. Credit and Borrowing

1. _____ is the provision of resources (such as granting a loan) by one party to another party where that second party does not reimburse the first party immediately, thereby generating a debt, and instead arranges either to repay or return those resources (or material(s) of equal value) at a later date. The first party is called a creditor, also known as a lender, while the second party is called a debtor, also known as a borrower.

Movements of financial capital are normally dependent on either _____ or equity transfers.

   a. Credit
   b. Warrant
   c. Comparable
   d. Clearing house

2. _____ or financing is to provide capital (funds), which means money for a project, a person, a business or any other private or public institutions.

Those funds can be allocated for either short term or long term purposes. The health fund is a new way of _____ private healthcare centers.

   a. Funding
   b. Proxy fight
   c. Product life cycle
   d. Synthetic CDO

3. _____, in bookkeeping, refers to assets, liabilities, income, and expenses recorded on individual pages of the so called book of final entry or ledger. Changes in _____ value are made by chronologically posting debit (DR) and credit (CR) entries to its page. Examples of _____s are cash, _____s receivable, mortgages, loans, land and buildings, common stock, sales, services provided, wages, and payroll overhead.
   a. Account
   b. Option
   c. Alpha
   d. Accretion

4. _____ is a fee paid on borrowed assets. It is the price paid for the use of borrowed money , or, money earned by deposited funds . Assets that are sometimes lent with _____ include money, shares, consumer goods through hire purchase, major assets such as aircraft, and even entire factories in finance lease arrangements.
   a. Insolvency
   b. Interest
   c. AAB
   d. A Random Walk Down Wall Street

Chapter 12. Credit and Borrowing

5. An _____ is the price a borrower pays for the use of money they do not own, and the return a lender receives for deferring the use of funds, by lending it to the borrower. _____s are normally expressed as a percentage rate over the period of one year.

    _____s targets are also a vital tool of monetary policy and are used to control variables like investment, inflation, and unemployment.

    a. A Random Walk Down Wall Street
    b. ABN Amro
    c. AAB
    d. Interest rate

6. The terms _____ , nominal _____ , and effective _____ describe the interest rate for a whole year (annualized), rather than just a monthly fee/rate, as applied on a loan, mortgage, credit card, etc. Those terms have formal, legal definitions in some countries or legal jurisdictions, but in general:

    - The nominal _____ is the simple-interest rate (for a year.)
    - The effective _____ is the fee+compound interest rate (calculated across a year.)

    The nominal _____ is calculated as: the rate, for a payment period, multiplied by the number of payment periods in a year. However, the exact legal definition of 'effective _____' can vary greatly in each jurisdiction, depending on the type of fees included, such as participation fees, loan origination fees, monthly service charges, or late fees. The effective _____ has been called the 'mathematically-true' interest rate for each year. The computation for the effective _____, as the fee+compound interest rate, can also vary depending on whether the up-front fees, such as origination or participation fees, are added to the entire amount, or treated as a short-term loan due in the first payment.

    a. A Random Walk Down Wall Street
    b. AAB
    c. ABN Amro
    d. Annual percentage rate

7. A _____ (U.S.), or credit reference agency (UK) is a company that collects information from various sources and provides consumer credit information on individual consumers for a variety of uses. This helps lenders assess credit worthiness, the ability to pay back a loan, and can affect the interest rate and other terms of a loan. Interest rates are not the same for everyone, but instead can be based on risk-based pricing, a form of price discrimination based on the different expected risks of different borrowers, as set out in their credit rating.

Chapter 12. Credit and Borrowing

a. Wall Street Journal prime rate
b. Credit bureau
c. Reserve requirement
d. Probability of default

8. _____ or credit report is, in many countries, a record of an individual's or company's past borrowing and repaying, including information about late payments and bankruptcy. The term 'credit reputation' can either be used synonymous to _____ or to credit score.

In the U.S., when a customer fills out an application for credit from a bank, store or credit card company, their information is forwarded to a credit bureau.

a. Promissory note
b. Financial plan
c. Credit repair software
d. Credit history

9. A '_____' is a 'Charge' that is paid to obtain the right to delay a payment. Essentially, the payer purchases the right to make a given payment in the future instead of in the Present. The '_____', or 'Charge' that must be paid to delay the payment, is simply the difference between what the payment amount would be if it were paid in the present and what the payment amount would be paid if it were paid in the future.
a. Risk modeling
b. Risk aversion
c. Value at risk
d. Discount

10. In economics, business, and accounting, a _____ is the value of money that has been used up to produce something, and hence is not available for use anymore. In business, the _____ may be one of acquisition, in which case the amount of money expended to acquire it is counted as _____. In this case, money is the input that is gone in order to acquire the thing.
a. Fixed costs
b. Marginal cost
c. Sliding scale fees
d. Cost

11. Credit insurance is a term used to describe both trade credit insurance and _____.

Chapter 12. Credit and Borrowing

_____ is a consumer purchase, often sold with a big ticket purchase such as an automobile. The insurance will pay off the loan balance in the event of the death or the disability of the borrower.

a. 7-Eleven
b. Credit life insurance
c. 4-4-5 Calendar
d. 529 plan

12. _____, refers to consumption opportunity gained by an entity within a specified time frame, which is generally expressed in monetary terms. However, for households and individuals, '_____ is the sum of all the wages, salaries, profits, interests payments, rents and other forms of earnings received... in a given period of time.' For firms, _____ generally refers to net-profit: what remains of revenue after expenses have been subtracted.

a. Annual report
b. Accrual
c. OIBDA
d. Income

13. _____ is a term used in the context of the purchase of expensive items such as a car and a house, whereby the payment is the initial upfront portion of the total amount due and it is usually given in cash at the time of finalizing the transaction. A loan is then required to make the full payment.

The main purpose of a _____ is to ensure that the lending institution can recover the balance due on the loan in the event that the borrower defaults.

a. Down payment
b. Royalties
c. Financial Institutions Reform Recovery and Enforcement Act
d. Business valuation

14. _____ refers to the replacement of an existing debt obligation with a debt obligation bearing different terms. The most common consumer _____ is for a home mortgage.

_____ may be undertaken to reduce interest rate/interest costs (by _____ at a lower rate), to extend the repayment time, to pay off other debt(s), to reduce one's periodic payment obligations (sometimes by taking a longer-term loan), to reduce or alter risk (such as by _____ from a variable-rate to a fixed-rate loan), and/or to raise cash for investment, consumption, or the payment of a dividend.

a. 4-4-5 Calendar
b. 529 plan
c. Refinancing
d. 7-Eleven

15. In finance, the _____ of a financial asset measures the sensitivity of the asset's price to interest rate movements, expressed as a number of years. The reason for expressing this sensitivity in years is that the time that will elapse until a cash flow is received allows more interest to accumulate. Therefore the price of an asset with long term cashflows has more interest rate sensitivity than an asset with cashflows in the near future.
   a. Yield to maturity
   b. Macaulay duration
   c. 4-4-5 Calendar
   d. Duration

16. A _____ is any credit facility extended to a business by a bank or financial institution. A _____ may take several forms such as cash credit, overdraft, demand loan, export packing credit, term loan, discounting or purchase of commercial bills etc. It is like an account that can readily be tapped into if the need arises or not touched at all and saved for emergencies.
   a. Debt-snowball method
   b. Line of credit
   c. Cash credit
   d. Default Notice

17. _____ is the value of a homeowner's unencumbered interest in their property, i.e. the difference between the home's fair market value and the unpaid balance of the mortgage and any outstanding debt over the home. _____ increases as the mortgage is paid or as the property enjoys appreciation. This is sometimes called real property value in economics.
   a. Real Estate Investment Trust
   b. Liquidation value
   c. REIT
   d. Home equity

18. The phrase _____ or bullet payment refers to one of two ways for repaying a loan; the other type is called amortizing payment or Amortization (business).

With a balloon loan, a _____ is paid back when the loan comes to its contractual maturity, e.g. reaches the deadline set to repayment at the time the loan was granted, representing the full loan amount (also called principal.) Periodic interest payments are generally made throughout the life of the loan.

a. Present value of costs
b. Refinancing risk
c. Future-oriented
d. Balloon payment

19. In lending agreements, _____ is a borrower's pledge of specific property to a lender, to secure repayment of a loan. The _____ serves as protection for a lender against a borrower's risk of default - that is, a borrower failing to pay the principal and interest under the terms of a loan obligation. If a borrower does default on a loan (due to insolvency or other event), that borrower forfeits (gives up) the property pledged as _____ *ollateral* - and the lender then becomes the owner of the _____.
  a. Future-oriented
  b. Refinancing risk
  c. Collateral
  d. Nominal value

20. _____ or amalgamation is the act of merging many things into one. In business, it often refers to the mergers or acquisitions of many smaller companies into much larger ones. The financial accounting term of _____ refers to the aggregated financial statements of a group company as consolidated account.
  a. Consolidation
  b. Cost of goods sold
  c. Write-off
  d. Retained earnings

21. A _____ is a person or body that offers unsecured loans at high interest rates to individuals, often backed by blackmail or threats of violence.

In much of history, usury laws made _____s commonplace. Many moneylenders skirted between legal and extra-legal activity.

  a. Cash credit
  b. Debt-snowball method
  c. Line of credit
  d. Loan shark

22. _____ is a legally declared inability or impairment of ability of an individual or organization to pay their creditors. Creditors may file a _____ petition against a debtor ('involuntary _____') in an effort to recoup a portion of what they are owed or initiate a restructuring. In the majority of cases, however, _____ is initiated by the debtor (a 'voluntary _____' that is filed by the bankrupt individual or organization.)

a. Bankruptcy
b. 529 plan
c. Debt settlement
d. 4-4-5 Calendar

23. In finance, a _____ is a debt security, in which the authorized issuer owes the holders a debt and, depending on the terms of the _____, is obliged to pay interest (the coupon) and/or to repay the principal at a later date, termed maturity.

Thus a _____ is a loan: the issuer is the borrower, the _____ holder is the lender, and the coupon is the interest. _____s provide the borrower with external funds to finance long-term investments, or, in the case of government _____s, to finance current expenditure.

a. Convertible bond
b. Puttable bond
c. Catastrophe bonds
d. Bond

24. _____ is a political organization established in 2002 and dedicated to the protection of children from abuse, exploitation and neglect. It is a nonprofit, 501(c)(4) membership association with members in every U.S. state and 10 nations. _____ achieved great success in its first three years, winning legislative victories in eight state legislatures.

a. The Depository Trust ' Clearing Corporation
b. Ford Foundation
c. Protect
d. First Prudential Markets

Chapter 13. Making Your Money Grow: An Overview

1. A _____ is a bond issued by a corporation. The term is usually applied to longer-term debt instruments, generally with a maturity date falling at least a year after their issue date. (The term 'commercial paper' is sometimes used for instruments with a shorter maturity.)
   a. Serial bond
   b. Corporate bond
   c. Brady bonds
   d. Government bond

2. _____ refers to any type of investment that yields a regular (or fixed) return.

   For example, if you lend money to a borrower and the borrower has to pay interest once a month, you have been issued a fixed-income security. When a company does this, it is often called a bond or corporate bank debt (although preferred stock is also sometimes considered to be _____).

   a. 4-4-5 Calendar
   b. 529 plan
   c. Bond market
   d. Fixed income

3. In finance, the _____ is the global financial market for short-term borrowing and lending. It provides short-term liquidity funding for the global financial system. The _____ is where short-term obligations such as Treasury bills, commercial paper and bankers' acceptances are bought and sold.
   a. Money market
   b. Cramdown
   c. Consumer debt
   d. Debt-for-equity swap

4. _____ involves the purchase, ownership, management, rental and/or sale of real estate for profit. Improvement of realty property as part of a real estate investment strategy is generally considered to be a sub-specialty of _____ called real estate development. Real estate is an asset form with limited liquidity relative to other investments, it is also capital intensive (although capital may be gained through mortgage leverage) and is highly cash flow dependent.
   a. Tenancy
   b. Liquidation value
   c. Real Estate Investment Trust
   d. Real estate investing

5. A _____ is a private or public market for the trading of company stock and derivatives of company stock at an agreed price; these are securities listed on a stock exchange as well as those only traded privately.

Chapter 13. Making Your Money Grow: An Overview

The size of the world _____ is estimated at about $36.6 trillion US at the beginning of October 2008 . The world derivatives market has been estimated at about $480 trillion face or nominal value, 12 times the size of the entire world economy.

a. Adolph Coors
b. Stock market
c. Anton Gelonkin
d. Andrew Tobias

6. In finance, a _____ is a debt security, in which the authorized issuer owes the holders a debt and, depending on the terms of the _____, is obliged to pay interest (the coupon) and/or to repay the principal at a later date, termed maturity.

Thus a _____ is a loan: the issuer is the borrower, the _____ holder is the lender, and the coupon is the interest. _____s provide the borrower with external funds to finance long-term investments, or, in the case of government _____s, to finance current expenditure.

a. Convertible bond
b. Catastrophe bonds
c. Bond
d. Puttable bond

7. _____, refers to consumption opportunity gained by an entity within a specified time frame, which is generally expressed in monetary terms. However, for households and individuals, '_____ is the sum of all the wages, salaries, profits, interests payments, rents and other forms of earnings received... in a given period of time.' For firms, _____ generally refers to net-profit: what remains of revenue after expenses have been subtracted.

a. OIBDA
b. Accrual
c. Annual report
d. Income

8. _____ is a measure of the ability of a debtor to pay their debts as and when they fall due. It is usually expressed as a ratio or a percentage of current liabilities.

For a corporation with a published balance sheet there are various ratios used to calculate a measure of liquidity.

a. Invested capital
b. Operating leverage
c. Operating profit margin
d. Accounting liquidity

9. _____ (in a financial context) is the assumption of the risk of loss, in return for the uncertain possibility of a reward. Only if one may safely say that a particular position involves no risk may one say, strictly speaking, that such a position represents an 'investment.' Financial _____ involves the buying, holding, selling, and short-selling of stocks, bonds, commodities, currencies, collectibles, real estate, derivatives, or any valuable financial instrument to profit from fluctuations in its price as opposed to buying it for use or for income via methods such as dividends or interest. _____ represents one of four market roles in Western financial markets, distinct from hedging, long- or short-term investing, and arbitrage.
a. Market anomaly
b. Central Securities Depository
c. Forward market
d. Speculation

10. In the original and simplified sense, _____ were things of value, of uniform quality, that were produced in large quantities by many different producers; the items from each different producer are considered equivalent. It is the contract and this underlying standard that define the commodity, not any quality inherent in the product.

_____ exchanges include:

- Chicago Board of Trade
- Kansas City Board of Trade
- Euronext.liffe
- Kuala Lumpur Futures Exchange
- Bhatinda Om ' Oil Exchange
- London Metal Exchange
- New York Mercantile Exchange
- Multi Commodity Exchange
- Dalian Commodity Exchange

Markets for trading _____ can be very efficient, particularly if the division into pools matches demand segments. These markets will quickly respond to changes in supply and demand to find an equilibrium price and quantity.

a. 529 plan
b. 7-Eleven
c. 4-4-5 Calendar
d. Commodities

11. In finance, the term _____ describes the amount in cash that returns to the owners of a security. Normally it does not include the price variations, at the difference of the total return. _____ applies to various stated rates of return on stocks (common and preferred, and convertible), fixed income instruments (bonds, notes, bills, strips, zero coupon), and some other investment type insurance products (e.g. annuities.)
   a. 4-4-5 Calendar
   b. Yield to maturity
   c. Macaulay duration
   d. Yield

12. In finance, _____, also known as return on investment is the ratio of money gained or lost on an investment relative to the amount of money invested. The amount of money gained or lost may be referred to as interest, profit/loss, gain/loss, or net income/loss. The money invested may be referred to as the asset, capital, principal, or the cost basis of the investment.
   a. Rate of return
   b. Stock or scrip dividends
   c. Composiition of Creditors
   d. Doctrine of the Proper Law

13. The _____ on a portfolio of investments takes into account not only the capital appreciation on the portfolio, but also the income received on the portfolio. The income typically consists of interest, dividends, and securities lending fees. This contrasts with the price return, which takes into account only the capital gain on an investment.
   a. Profitability index
   b. Capitalization rate
   c. Total return
   d. Global tactical asset allocation

14. In finance, a _____ is a position established in one market in an attempt to offset exposure to the price risk of an equal but opposite obligation or position in another market -- usually, but not always, in the context of one's commercial activity. Hedging is a strategy designed to minimize exposure to such business risks as a sharp contraction in demand for one's inventory, while still allowing the business to profit from producing and maintaining that inventory. A typical hedger might be a farmer with 2000 acres of unharvested wheat in the ground, who would rather tend his crop without the distraction of uncertain prices.

Chapter 13. Making Your Money Grow: An Overview

a. 4-4-5 Calendar
b. 529 plan
c. 7-Eleven
d. Hedge

15. In economics, _____ is a rise in the general level of prices of goods and services in an economy over a period of time. The term '_____' once referred to increases in the money supply (monetary _____); however, economic debates about the relationship between money supply and price levels have led to its primary use today in describing price _____. _____ can also be described as a decline in the real value of money--a loss of purchasing power in the medium of exchange which is also the monetary unit of account.

a. AAB
b. ABN Amro
c. A Random Walk Down Wall Street
d. Inflation

16. In finance, the value of an option consists of two components, its intrinsic value and its _____. Time value is simply the difference between option value and intrinsic value. _____ is also known as theta, extrinsic value, or instrumental value.

a. Conservatism
b. Debt buyer
c. Global Squeeze
d. Time value

17. Simply put, _____ is the value of money figuring in a given amount of interest for a given amount of time. For example 100 dollars of todays money held for a year at 5 percent interest is worth 105 dollars, therefore 100 dollars paid now or 105 dollars paid exactly one year from now is the same amount of payment of money with that given intersest at that given amount of time. This notion dates at least to Martín de Azpilcueta of the School of Salamanca.

All of the standard calculations for _____ derive from the most basic algebraic expression for the present value of a future sum, 'discounted' to the present by an amount equal to the _____. For example, a sum of FV to be received in one year is discounted (at the rate of interest r) to give a sum of PV at present: $PV = FV -- r·PV = FV/(1+r)$.

a. Time value of money
b. Zero-coupon bond
c. Coefficient of variation
d. Current account

18. _____ measures the nominal future sum of money that a given sum of money is 'worth' at a specified time in the future assuming a certain interest rate rate of return; it is the present value multiplied by the accumulation function.

The value does not include corrections for inflation or other factors that affect the true value of money in the future. This is used in time value of money calculations.

   a. Discounted cash flow
   b. Future-oriented
   c. Present value of costs
   d. Future value

19. An _____ is a retirement plan account that provides some tax advantages for retirement savings in the United States.
   a. ABN Amro
   b. AAB
   c. A Random Walk Down Wall Street
   d. Individual Retirement Arrangement

20. _____, in bookkeeping, refers to assets, liabilities, income, and expenses recorded on individual pages of the so called book of final entry or ledger. Changes in _____ value are made by chronologically posting debit (DR) and credit (CR) entries to its page. Examples of _____s are cash, _____s receivable, mortgages, loans, land and buildings, common stock, sales, services provided, wages, and payroll overhead.
   a. Alpha
   b. Option
   c. Accretion
   d. Account

21. _____s are full-fledged pension plans for self-employed people in the United States. They are sometimes called HR10 plans and are not Individual Retirement Accounts (IRA.)

Since a _____ is a full-fledged pension, there is a Keogh for every employer-sponsored pension-plan design.

   a. 4-4-5 Calendar
   b. 7-Eleven
   c. 529 plan
   d. Keogh plan

22. A _____ is a pool of assets forming an independent legal entity that are bought with the contributions to a pension plan for the exclusive purpose of financing pension plan benefits.

_____s are important shareholders of listed and private companies. They are especially important to the stock market where large institutional investors like the Ontario Teachers' Pension Plan dominate.

   a. Pension fund
   b. Leveraged buyout
   c. Leverage
   d. Limited liability company

23. _____ is a fee paid on borrowed assets. It is the price paid for the use of borrowed money, or, money earned by deposited funds. Assets that are sometimes lent with _____ include money, shares, consumer goods through hire purchase, major assets such as aircraft, and even entire factories in finance lease arrangements.
   a. AAB
   b. A Random Walk Down Wall Street
   c. Insolvency
   d. Interest

24. An _____ is the price a borrower pays for the use of money they do not own, and the return a lender receives for deferring the use of funds, by lending it to the borrower. _____s are normally expressed as a percentage rate over the period of one year.

_____s targets are also a vital tool of monetary policy and are used to control variables like investment, inflation, and unemployment.

   a. AAB
   b. Interest rate
   c. ABN Amro
   d. A Random Walk Down Wall Street

25. In financial accounting, the term _____ is most commonly used to describe any part of shareholders' equity, except for basic share capital. Sometimes, the term is used instead of the term provision; such a use, however, is inconsistent with the terminology suggested by International Accounting Standards Board. For more information about provisions, see provision (accounting.)

a. Treasury stock
b. Closing entries
c. FIFO and LIFO accounting
d. Reserve

26. The terms _____ , nominal _____, and effective _____ describe the interest rate for a whole year (annualized), rather than just a monthly fee/rate, as applied on a loan, mortgage, credit card, etc. Those terms have formal, legal definitions in some countries or legal jurisdictions, but in general:

- The nominal _____ is the simple-interest rate (for a year.)
- The effective _____ is the fee+compound interest rate (calculated across a year.)

The nominal _____ is calculated as: the rate, for a payment period, multiplied by the number of payment periods in a year. However, the exact legal definition of 'effective _____' can vary greatly in each jurisdiction, depending on the type of fees included, such as participation fees, loan origination fees, monthly service charges, or late fees. The effective _____ has been called the 'mathematically-true' interest rate for each year. The computation for the effective _____, as the fee+compound interest rate, can also vary depending on whether the up-front fees, such as origination or participation fees, are added to the entire amount, or treated as a short-term loan due in the first payment.

a. Annual percentage rate
b. ABN Amro
c. A Random Walk Down Wall Street
d. AAB

Chapter 14. Making Your Money Grow: The Money Market

1. In finance, the _____ is the global financial market for short-term borrowing and lending. It provides short-term liquidity funding for the global financial system. The _____ is where short-term obligations such as Treasury bills, commercial paper and bankers' acceptances are bought and sold.
    a. Debt-for-equity swap
    b. Cramdown
    c. Consumer debt
    d. Money market

2. A _____ is a bond issued by a corporation. The term is usually applied to longer-term debt instruments, generally with a maturity date falling at least a year after their issue date. (The term 'commercial paper' is sometimes used for instruments with a shorter maturity.)
    a. Government bond
    b. Serial bond
    c. Brady bonds
    d. Corporate bond

3. In finance, a _____ is a debt security, in which the authorized issuer owes the holders a debt and, depending on the terms of the _____, is obliged to pay interest (the coupon) and/or to repay the principal at a later date, termed maturity.

    Thus a _____ is a loan: the issuer is the borrower, the _____ holder is the lender, and the coupon is the interest. _____s provide the borrower with external funds to finance long-term investments, or, in the case of government _____s, to finance current expenditure.

    a. Puttable bond
    b. Bond
    c. Catastrophe bonds
    d. Convertible bond

4. _____ is a fee paid on borrowed assets. It is the price paid for the use of borrowed money, or, money earned by deposited funds. Assets that are sometimes lent with _____ include money, shares, consumer goods through hire purchase, major assets such as aircraft, and even entire factories in finance lease arrangements.
    a. Insolvency
    b. AAB
    c. Interest
    d. A Random Walk Down Wall Street

Chapter 14. Making Your Money Grow: The Money Market

5. _____, in bookkeeping, refers to assets, liabilities, income, and expenses recorded on individual pages of the so called book of final entry or ledger. Changes in _____ value are made by chronologically posting debit (DR) and credit (CR) entries to its page. Examples of _____s are cash, _____s receivable, mortgages, loans, land and buildings, common stock, sales, services provided, wages, and payroll overhead.
   a. Option
   b. Account
   c. Alpha
   d. Accretion

6. A _____ s a time deposit, a financial product commonly offered to consumers by banks, thrift institutions, and credit unions.

They are similar to savings accounts in that they are insured and thus virtually risk-free; they are 'money in the bank'. They are different from savings accounts in that they have a specific, fixed term (often three months, six months, or one to five years), and, usually, a fixed interest rate.

   a. Reserve requirement
   b. Certificate of deposit
   c. Variable rate mortgage
   d. Time deposit

7. In the global money market, _____ is an unsecured promissory note with a fixed maturity of one to 270 days. _____ is a money-market security issued (sold) by large banks and corporations to get money to meet short term debt obligations (for example, payroll), and is only backed by an issuing bank or corporation's promise to pay the face amount on the maturity date specified on the note. Since it is not backed by collateral, only firms with excellent credit ratings from a recognized rating agency will be able to sell their _____ at a reasonable price.
   a. Book building
   b. Trade-off theory
   c. Commercial paper
   d. Financial distress

8. The coupon or _____ of a bond is the amount of interest paid per year expressed as a percentage of the face value of the bond.

For example if you hold $10,000 nominal of a bond described as a 4.5% loan stock, you will receive $450 in interest each year (probably in two installments of $225 each.)

Not all bonds have coupons.

a. Coupon rate
b. Puttable bond
c. Revenue bonds
d. Zero-coupon bond

9. The _____, interest yield, income yield, flat yield or running yield is a financial term used in reference to bonds and other fixed-interest securities such as gilts. It is the ratio of the annual interest payment and the bond's current price.

The _____ only therefore refers to the yield of the bond at the current moment. It does not reflect the total return over the life of the bond. In particular, it takes no account of reinvestment risk (the uncertainty about the rate at which future cashflows can be reinvested) or the fact that bonds usually mature at par value, which can be an important component of a bond's return.

a. Perpetuity
b. Modified Internal Rate of Return
c. Stochastic volatility
d. Current yield

10. In finance, the term _____ describes the amount in cash that returns to the owners of a security. Normally it does not include the price variations, at the difference of the total return. _____ applies to various stated rates of return on stocks (common and preferred, and convertible), fixed income instruments (bonds, notes, bills, strips, zero coupon), and some other investment type insurance products (e.g. annuities.)

a. 4-4-5 Calendar
b. Yield to maturity
c. Yield
d. Macaulay duration

11. The _____ or redemption yield is the yield promised to the bondholder on the assumption that the bond or other fixed-interest security such as gilts will be held to maturity, that all coupon and principal payments will be made and coupon payments are reinvested at the bond's promised yield at the same rate as invested. It is a measure of the return of the bond. This technique in theory allows investors to calculate the fair value of different financial instruments.

a. Macaulay duration
b. Yield
c. 4-4-5 Calendar
d. Yield to maturity

12. _____ is a life of security. It may also refer to the final payment date of a loan or other financial instrument, at which point all remaining interest and principal is due to be paid.

Chapter 14. Making Your Money Grow: The Money Market 75

1, 3, 6 months _____ band can be calculated by using 30-day per month periods.

   a. False billing
   b. Replacement cost
   c. Primary market
   d. Maturity

13. A _____ is a fund established by a government agency or business for the purpose of reducing debt.

The _____ was first used in Great Britain in the 18th century to reduce national debt. While used by Robert Walpole in 1716 and effectively in the 1720s and early 1730s, it originated in the commercial tax syndicates of the Italian peninsula of the 14th century to retire redeemable public debt of those cities.

   a. Debtor
   b. Security interest
   c. Modern portfolio theory
   d. Sinking fund

14. In finance, a _____ is a position established in one market in an attempt to offset exposure to the price risk of an equal but opposite obligation or position in another market -- usually, but not always, in the context of one's commercial activity. Hedging is a strategy designed to minimize exposure to such business risks as a sharp contraction in demand for one's inventory, while still allowing the business to profit from producing and maintaining that inventory. A typical hedger might be a farmer with 2000 acres of unharvested wheat in the ground, who would rather tend his crop without the distraction of uncertain prices.
   a. 4-4-5 Calendar
   b. 529 plan
   c. 7-Eleven
   d. Hedge

15. In finance, a _____ (non-investment grade bond, speculative grade bond or junk bond) is a bond that is rated below investment grade at the time of purchase. These bonds have a higher risk of default or other adverse credit events, but typically pay higher yields than better quality bonds in order to make them attractive to investors.
   a. Volatility
   b. Sharpe ratio
   c. Private equity
   d. High yield bond

Chapter 14. Making Your Money Grow: The Money Market

16. _____ is a measure of the ability of a debtor to pay their debts as and when they fall due. It is usually expressed as a ratio or a percentage of current liabilities.

For a corporation with a published balance sheet there are various ratios used to calculate a measure of liquidity.

   a. Accounting liquidity
   b. Operating profit margin
   c. Operating leverage
   d. Invested capital

17. A _____ is defined as a certificate of agreement of loans which is given under the company's stamp and carries an undertaking that the _____ holder will get a fixed return (fixed on the basis of interest rates) and the principal amount whenever the _____ matures.

In finance, a _____ is a long-term debt instrument used by governments and large companies to obtain funds. It is defined as 'a debt secured only by the debtor's earning power, not by a lien on any specific asset.' It is similar to a bond except the securitization conditions are different.

   a. Partial Payment
   b. Collateral Management
   c. Collection agency
   d. Debenture

18. _____ are government bonds issued by the United States Department of the Treasury through the Bureau of the Public Debt. They are the debt financing instruments of the U.S. Federal government, and they are often referred to simply as Treasuries or Treasurys. There are four types of marketable _____: Treasury bills, Treasury notes, Treasury bonds, and Treasury Inflation Protected Securities (TIPS.)
   a. Treasury securities
   b. Treasury Inflation-Protected Securities
   c. Treasury Inflation Protected Securities
   d. 4-4-5 Calendar

19. A _____ is a bond issued by a national government denominated in the country's own currency. Bonds issued by national governments in foreign currencies are normally referred to as sovereign bonds. The first ever _____ was issued by the British government in 1693 to raise money to fund a war against France.

a. Municipal bond
b. Zero-coupon bond
c. Collateralized debt obligations
d. Government Bond

20. Accrual, in accounting, describes the accounting method known as _____, whereby revenues and expenses are recognized when they are accrued, i.e. accumulated (earned or incurred), regardless when the actual cash is received or paid out.

E.g. a company delivers a product to a customer who will pay for it 30 days later in the next fiscal year starting a week after the delivery. The company recognizes the proceeds as a revenue in its current income statement still for the fiscal year of the delivery, even though it will get paid in cash during the following accounting period.

a. Accrual basis
b. AAB
c. A Random Walk Down Wall Street
d. ABN Amro

21. A _____ is a fungible, negotiable instrument representing financial value. They are broadly categorized into debt securities (such as banknotes, bonds and debentures), and equity securities; e.g., common stocks. The company or other entity issuing the _____ is called the issuer.

a. Securities lending
b. Book entry
c. Tracking stock
d. Security

22. A _____ is a bond bought at a price lower than its face value, with the face value repaid at the time of maturity. It does not make periodic interest payments, or so-called 'coupons,' hence the term zero-coupon bond. Investors earn return from the compounded interest all paid at maturity plus the difference between the discounted price of the bond and its par value.

a. Bowie bonds
b. Callable bond
c. Municipal bond
d. Zero coupon bond

23. A _____ is a legal pledge in United States municipal finance, in which an entity pledges its full faith and credit to repay its debt, typically a _____ bond.

a. Covenant
b. General obligation
c. Financial Institutions Reform Recovery and Enforcement Act
d. Letter of credit

24. An _____ is a retirement plan account that provides some tax advantages for retirement savings in the United States.

a. AAB
b. ABN Amro
c. Individual Retirement Arrangement
d. A Random Walk Down Wall Street

25. In the United States, a _____ is a bond issued by a city or other local government, or their agencies. Potential issuers of these bonds include cities, counties, redevelopment agencies, school districts, publicly owned airports and seaports, and any other governmental entity (or group of governments) below the state level. They may be general obligations of the issuer or secured by specified revenues.

a. Puttable bond
b. Senior debt
c. Municipal bond
d. Premium bond

26. In business, _____ is income that a company receives from its normal business activities, usually from the sale of goods and services to customers. Some companies also receive _____ from interest, dividends or royalties paid to them by other companies. _____ may refer to business income in general, or it may refer to the amount, in a monetary unit, received during a period of time, as in 'Last year, Company X had _____ of $32 million.'

In many countries, including the UK, _____ is referred to as turnover.

a. Furniture, Fixtures and Equipment
b. Matching principle
c. Revenue
d. Bottom line

27. _____ are bonds issued by governments, authorities, or public benefit corporations that are guaranteed by the revenue flow of the issuing agency.

Chapter 14. Making Your Money Grow: The Money Market

The Supreme Court decision of Pollock versus Farmer's Loan and Trust Company of 1895 initiated a wave or series of innovations for the financial services community in both tax-treatment and regulation from government. This specific case, according to a leading investment bank's research, resulted in the 'intergovernmental tax immunity doctrine,' ultimately leading to 'tax-free status.' Municipal bonds are generally exempt from federal tax on their interest payments (not capital gains.)

   a. Callable bond
   b. Gilts
   c. Private activity bond
   d. Revenue bonds

28. A _____ is an exemption from all or certain taxes of a state or nation in which part of the taxes that would normally be collected from an individual or an organization are instead foregone.

Normally a _____ is provided to an individual or organization which falls within a class which the government wishes to promote economically, such as charitable organizations. _____s are usually meant to either reduce the tax burden on a particular segment of society in the interests of fairness or to promote some type of economic activity through reducing the tax burden on those organizations or individuals who are involved in that activity.

   a. Tax compliance solution
   b. Tax incidence
   c. Federal Open Market Committee
   d. Tax exemption

29. A _____, is a collective investment scheme with a limited number of shares.

New shares are rarely issued after the fund is launched; shares are not normally redeemable for cash or securities until the fund liquidates. Typically an investor can acquire shares in a _____ by buying shares on a secondary market from a broker, market maker, or other investor as opposed to an open-end fund where all transactions eventually involve the fund company creating new shares on the fly (in exchange for either cash or securities) or redeeming shares (for cash or securities.)

   a. Closed-end fund
   b. Money market funds
   c. Stock fund
   d. Mutual fund fees and expenses

Chapter 14. Making Your Money Grow: The Money Market

30. A _____ is a professionally managed type of collective investment scheme that pools money from many investors and invests it in stocks, bonds, short-term money market instruments, and/or other securities. The _____ will have a fund manager that trades the pooled money on a regular basis. Currently, the worldwide value of all _____s totals more than $26 trillion.

Since 1940, there have been three basic types of investment companies in the United States: open-end funds, also known in the US as _____s; unit investment trusts (UITs); and closed-end funds.

    a. Financial intermediary
    b. Net asset value
    c. Trust company
    d. Mutual fund

31. A _____ is a form of collective investment constituted under a trust deed.

Found in Australia, Ireland, the Isle of Man, Jersey, New Zealand, South Africa, Singapore, and the UK, _____s offer access to a wide range of securities.

_____s are open-ended investments; therefore the underlying value of the assets is always directly represented by the total number of units issued multiplied by the unit price less the transaction or management fee charged and any other associated costs.

    a. AAB
    b. A Random Walk Down Wall Street
    c. ABN Amro
    d. Unit trust

32. _____ or financing is to provide capital (funds), which means money for a project, a person, a business or any other private or public institutions.

Those funds can be allocated for either short term or long term purposes. The health fund is a new way of _____ private healthcare centers.

    a. Synthetic CDO
    b. Funding
    c. Product life cycle
    d. Proxy fight

Chapter 14. Making Your Money Grow: The Money Market

33. A _____ is a pool of assets forming an independent legal entity that are bought with the contributions to a pension plan for the exclusive purpose of financing pension plan benefits.

_____s are important shareholders of listed and private companies. They are especially important to the stock market where large institutional investors like the Ontario Teachers' Pension Plan dominate.

   a. Leverage
   b. Leveraged buyout
   c. Pension fund
   d. Limited liability company

34. _____ involves the purchase, ownership, management, rental and/or sale of real estate for profit. Improvement of realty property as part of a real estate investment strategy is generally considered to be a sub-specialty of _____ called real estate development. Real estate is an asset form with limited liquidity relative to other investments, it is also capital intensive (although capital may be gained through mortgage leverage) and is highly cash flow dependent.
   a. Tenancy
   b. Real estate investing
   c. Real Estate Investment Trust
   d. Liquidation value

35. A _____ is a private or public market for the trading of company stock and derivatives of company stock at an agreed price; these are securities listed on a stock exchange as well as those only traded privately.

The size of the world _____ is estimated at about $36.6 trillion US at the beginning of October 2008 . The world derivatives market has been estimated at about $480 trillion face or nominal value, 12 times the size of the entire world economy.

   a. Anton Gelonkin
   b. Adolph Coors
   c. Andrew Tobias
   d. Stock market

36. In finance, a _____ is a type of bond that can be converted into shares of stock in the issuing company, usually at some pre-announced ratio. It is a hybrid security with debt- and equity-like features. Although it typically has a low coupon rate, the holder is compensated with the ability to convert the bond to common stock, usually at a substantial discount to the stock's market value.

a. Corporate bond
b. Bond fund
c. Gilts
d. Convertible bond

37. In finance, _____, also known as return on investment is the ratio of money gained or lost on an investment relative to the amount of money invested. The amount of money gained or lost may be referred to as interest, profit/loss, gain/loss, or net income/loss. The money invested may be referred to as the asset, capital, principal, or the cost basis of the investment.
   a. Composiition of Creditors
   b. Doctrine of the Proper Law
   c. Stock or scrip dividends
   d. Rate of return

Chapter 15. Making Your Money Grow: The Stock Market

1. A _____ is a private or public market for the trading of company stock and derivatives of company stock at an agreed price; these are securities listed on a stock exchange as well as those only traded privately.

The size of the world _____ is estimated at about $36.6 trillion US at the beginning of October 2008 . The world derivatives market has been estimated at about $480 trillion face or nominal value, 12 times the size of the entire world economy.

   a. Anton Gelonkin
   b. Stock market
   c. Adolph Coors
   d. Andrew Tobias

2. _____ is that which is owed; usually referencing assets owed, but the term can cover other obligations. In the case of assets, _____ is a means of using future purchasing power in the present before a summation has been earned. Some companies and corporations use _____ as a part of their overall corporate finance strategy.
   a. Credit cycle
   b. Partial Payment
   c. Cross-collateralization
   d. Debt

3. _____, is when a company issues common stock or shares to the public for the first time. They are often issued by smaller, younger companies seeking capital to expand, but can also be done by large privately-owned companies looking to become publicly traded.

In an _____ the issuer may obtain the assistance of an underwriting firm, which helps it determine what type of security to issue (common or preferred), best offering price and time to bring it to market.

   a. Asian Financial Crisis
   b. Insolvency
   c. Interest
   d. Initial public offering

4. The institution most often referenced by the word '_____' is a public or publicly traded _____, the shares of which are traded on a public stock exchange (e.g., the New York Stock Exchange or Nasdaq in the United States) where shares of stock of _____s are bought and sold by and to the general public. Most of the largest businesses in the world are publicly traded _____s. However, the majority of _____s are said to be closely held, privately held or close _____s, meaning that no ready market exists for the trading of shares.

Chapter 15. Making Your Money Grow: The Stock Market

a. Federal Home Loan Mortgage Corporation
b. Depository Trust Company
c. Protect
d. Corporation

5. In business and finance, a _____ (also referred to as equity _____) of stock means a _____ of ownership in a corporation (company.) In the plural, stocks is often used as a synonym for _____s especially in the United States, but it is less commonly used that way outside of North America.

In the United Kingdom, South Africa, and Australia, stock can also refer to completely different financial instruments such as government bonds or, less commonly, to all kinds of marketable securities.

a. Margin
b. Bucket shop
c. Procter ' Gamble
d. Share

6. In corporate law, a _____ is a legal document that certifies ownership of a specific number of stock shares in a corporation. In large corporations, buying shares does not always lead to a _____

Usually only shareholders with _____s can vote in a shareholders' general meeting.

a. 7-Eleven
b. 529 plan
c. 4-4-5 Calendar
d. Stock certificate

7. A _____, securities exchange or (in Europe) bourse is a corporation or mutual organization which provides 'trading' facilities for stock brokers and traders, to trade stocks and other securities. _____s also provide facilities for the issue and redemption of securities as well as other financial instruments and capital events including the payment of income and dividends. The securities traded on a _____ include: shares issued by companies, unit trusts and other pooled investment products and bonds.

a. 7-Eleven
b. 4-4-5 Calendar
c. 529 plan
d. Stock exchange

Chapter 15. Making Your Money Grow: The Stock Market

8. A _____ is a fungible, negotiable instrument representing financial value. They are broadly categorized into debt securities (such as banknotes, bonds and debentures), and equity securities; e.g., common stocks. The company or other entity issuing the _____ is called the issuer.
   a. Book entry
   b. Tracking stock
   c. Securities lending
   d. Security

9. The U.S. _____ is an independent agency of the United States government which holds primary responsibility for enforcing the federal securities laws and regulating the securities industry, the nation's stock and options exchanges, and other electronic securities markets. The SEC was created by section 4 of the SEC of 1934 (now codified as 15 U.S.C. Â§ 78d and commonly referred to as the 1934 Act.)
   a. 4-4-5 Calendar
   b. 529 plan
   c. 7-Eleven
   d. Securities and Exchange Commission

10. The _____ is a federally mandated non-profit corporation in the United States that protects securities investors from harm if a broker-dealer company fails. Investors are not insured for any potential loss while invested in the market.

    Congress created _____ in 1970 through the _____ (15 U.S.C.

    a. SIPC
    b. Williams Act
    c. Prudent man rule
    d. Rule 144A

11. Companies that have publicly traded securities typically use _____ to keep track of the individuals and entities that own their stocks and bonds. Most _____ are banks or trust companies, but sometimes a company acts as its own transfer agent.

_____ perform three main functions:

1. Issue and cancel certificates to reflect changes in ownership. For example, when a company declares a stock dividend or stock split, the transfer agent issues new shares. _____ keep records of who owns a company's stocks and bonds and how those stocks and bonds are held--whether by the owner in certificate form, by the company in book-entry form, or by the investor's brokerage firm in street name. They also keep records of how many shares or bonds each investor owns.
2. Act as an intermediary for the company. A transfer agent may also serve as the company's paying agent to pay out interest, cash and stock dividends, or other distributions to stock- and bondholders. In addition, _____ act as proxy agent (sending out proxy materials), exchange agent (exchanging a company's stock or bonds in a merger), tender agent (tendering shares in a tender offer), and mailing agent (mailing the company's quarterly, annual, and other reports.)
3. Handle lost, destroyed, or stolen certificates. _____ help shareholders and bondholders when a stock or bond certificate has been lost, destroyed, or stolen.

In many cases, you can find out which transfer agent a company uses by visiting the investor relations section of the company's website.

a. Transfer agents
b. 7-Eleven
c. 4-4-5 Calendar
d. 529 plan

12. A _____ or a stock investor is an individual or firm who buys and sells stocks or bonds (and possibly other financial assets) in the financial markets. Charting is the use of graphical and analytical patterns and data to attempt to predict future prices.

Individuals or firms trading equity (stock) on the stock markets as their principal capacity are called _____s. Stock traders usually try to profit from short-term price volatility with trades lasting anywhere from several seconds to several weeks.

a. Stock or scrip dividends
b. Lookback options
c. Rate of return
d. Stock trader

13. A _____ is an order to buy a security at no more (or sell at no less) than a specific price. This gives the customer some control over the price at which the trade is executed, but may prevent the order from being executed ('filled'.)

A buy _____ can only be executed by the broker at the limit price or lower.

Chapter 15. Making Your Money Grow: The Stock Market

a. Commercial mortgage-backed securities
b. Common stock
c. Block premium
d. Limit order

14. A _____ is a buy or sell order to be executed by the broker immediately at current market prices. As long as there are willing sellers and buyers, _____s are filled.

A _____ is the simplest of the order types.

a. Stockholder
b. Block premium
c. Trading curb
d. Market order

15. In economic models, the _____ time frame assumes no fixed factors of production. Firms can enter or leave the marketplace, and the cost (and availability) of land, labor, raw materials, and capital goods can be assumed to vary. In contrast, in the short-run time frame, certain factors are assumed to be fixed, because there is not sufficient time for them to change.

a. Short-run
b. 4-4-5 Calendar
c. 529 plan
d. Long-run

16. In economics, the concept of the _____ refers to the decision-making time frame of a firm in which at least one factor of production is fixed. Costs which are fixed in the _____ have no impact on a firms decisions. For example a firm can raise output by increasing the amount of labour through overtime.

a. 4-4-5 Calendar
b. Long-run
c. 529 plan
d. Short-run

17. _____ is commonly defined as the amount of a company's or a person's income before all deductions or any taxpayer's income, except that which is specifically excluded by the Internal Revenue Code, before taking deductions or taxes into account. For a business, this amount is pre-tax net sales less cost of sales. Section 61 of the Internal Revenue Code (Code) defines '_____' as 'all income from whatever source derived.' Section 61(a) of the Code lists fifteen examples of items included in _____; however, the list is not exhaustive.

Chapter 15. Making Your Money Grow: The Stock Market

a. Second lien loan
b. Financial distress
c. Shareholder value
d. Gross income

18. _____, refers to consumption opportunity gained by an entity within a specified time frame, which is generally expressed in monetary terms. However, for households and individuals, '_____ is the sum of all the wages, salaries, profits, interests payments, rents and other forms of earnings received... in a given period of time.' For firms, _____ generally refers to net-profit: what remains of revenue after expenses have been subtracted.
    a. Annual report
    b. OIBDA
    c. Accrual
    d. Income

19. _____ is casually defined as the use of computers in stock markets to engage in arbitrage and portfolio insurance strategies. However, the New York Stock Exchange (NYSE) defines the term as 'a wide range of portfolio trading strategies involving the purchase or sale of 15 or more stocks having a total market value of $1 million or more' without any direct reference to the use of computers. The word 'program' can be interpreted in its earlier, more general meaning of a defined and pre-arranged sequence of steps, rather than specifically a computer program.
    a. Stop order
    b. Wash sale
    c. Share price
    d. Program trading

20. _____ is a security analysis discipline for forecasting the future direction of prices through the study of past market data, primarily price and volume. In its purest form, _____ considers only the actual price and volume behavior of the market or instrument. Technical analysts may employ models and trading rules based on price and volume transformations, such as the relative strength index, moving averages, regressions, inter-market and intra-market price correlations, cycles or, classically, through recognition of chart patterns.
    a. Support and resistance
    b. Dow theory
    c. Point and figure
    d. Technical analysis

21. A _____ is a payment made by a corporation to its shareholder members. When a corporation earns a profit or surplus, that money can be put to two uses: it can either be re-invested in the business (called retained earnings), or it can be paid to the shareholders as a _____. Many corporations retain a portion of their earnings and pay the remainder as a _____.

a. Dividend yield
b. Dividend
c. Dividend puzzle
d. Special dividend

22. In finance, the term _____ describes the amount in cash that returns to the owners of a security. Normally it does not include the price variations, at the difference of the total return. _____ applies to various stated rates of return on stocks (common and preferred, and convertible), fixed income instruments (bonds, notes, bills, strips, zero coupon), and some other investment type insurance products (e.g. annuities.)
   a. Macaulay duration
   b. Yield
   c. 4-4-5 Calendar
   d. Yield to maturity

23. In finance, a _____ is a debt security, in which the authorized issuer owes the holders a debt and, depending on the terms of the _____, is obliged to pay interest (the coupon) and/or to repay the principal at a later date, termed maturity.

Thus a _____ is a loan: the issuer is the borrower, the _____ holder is the lender, and the coupon is the interest. _____s provide the borrower with external funds to finance long-term investments, or, in the case of government _____s, to finance current expenditure.

   a. Puttable bond
   b. Catastrophe bonds
   c. Convertible bond
   d. Bond

24. _____ is a form of corporation equity ownership represented in the securities. It is dangerous in comparison to preferred shares and some other investment options, in that in the event of bankruptcy, _____ investors receive their funds after preferred stockholders, bondholders, creditors, etc. On the other hand, common shares on average perform better than preferred shares or bonds over time.
   a. Stop-limit order
   b. Stock market bubble
   c. Stock split
   d. Common stock

Chapter 15. Making Your Money Grow: The Stock Market

25. The _____ is one of several stock market indices, created by nineteenth-century Wall Street Journal editor and Dow Jones ' Company co-founder Charles Dow. Dow compiled the index to gauge the performance of the industrial sector of the American stock market. It is the second-oldest U.S. market index, after the Dow Jones Transportation Average, which Dow also created.
   a. 529 plan
   b. 7-Eleven
   c. 4-4-5 Calendar
   d. Dow Jones Industrial Average

26. The _____ is a stock exchange based in New York City, New York. It is the largest stock exchange in the world by dollar value of its listed companies securities. As of October 2008, the combined capitalization of all domestic _____ listed companies was $10.1 trillion.
   a. 529 plan
   b. 4-4-5 Calendar
   c. 7-Eleven
   d. New York Stock Exchange

27. A _____ is a normalized average (typically a weighted average) of prices for a given class of goods or services in a given region, during a given interval of time. It is a statistic designed to help to compare how these prices, taken as a whole, differ between time periods or geographical locations.
   a. Price discrimination
   b. Price index
   c. Discounts and allowances
   d. Transfer pricing

28. A _____ is a method of measuring a section of the stock market. Many indices are cited by news or financial services firms and are used to benchmark the performance of portfolios such as mutual funds.
   a. Program trading
   b. Stop order
   c. Trading curb
   d. Stock market index

29. A _____ is the price of a single share of a no. of saleable stocks of the company. Once the stock is purchased, the owner becomes a shareholder of the company that issued the share.

a. Trading curb
b. Share price
c. Stock split
d. Whisper numbers

30. In finance, _____ are stocks that appreciate in value and yield a high return on equity (ROE.) Analysts compute ROE by taking the company's net income and dividing it by the company's equity. To be classified as a growth stock, analysts expect to see at least 15 percent return on equity.
a. Stock valuation
b. 4-4-5 Calendar
c. Security Analysis
d. Growth stocks

31. _____ is a type of private equity capital typically provided to early-stage, high-potential, growth companies in the interest of generating a return through an eventual realization event such as an IPO or trade sale of the company. _____ investments are generally made as cash in exchange for shares in the invested company. It is typical for _____ investors to identify and back companies in high technology industries such as biotechnology and ICT.
a. Treasury Inflation-Protected Securities
b. Probability distribution
c. Tail risk
d. Venture capital

32. A mutual shareholder or _____ is an individual or company (including a corporation) that legally owns one or more shares of stock in a joint stock company. A company's shareholders collectively own that company. Thus, the typical goal of such companies is to enhance shareholder value.
a. Limit order
b. Trading curb
c. Stock market bubble
d. Stockholder

33. A _____ is an equity investment option offered directly from the underlying company. The investor does not receive quarterly dividends directly as cash; instead, the investor's dividends are directly reinvested in the underlying equity. It should be noted that the investor still must pay tax annually on his or her dividend income, whether it is received or reinvested.

a. Dividend puzzle
b. Dividend decision
c. Dividend payout ratio
d. Dividend reinvestment plan

34. The key date to remember for dividend paying stocks is the _____. The _____ is different from the record date. The _____ is typically two trading days before the record date.

In order to receive the upcoming dividend payment payout, you must already own or you must purchase the stock prior to the _____. It is important to note that in most countries, when you buy or sell any stock, there is a three trading-day settlement period on your order.

a. Index number
b. Asian Financial Crisis
c. Ex-dividend date
d. Insolvency

35. It is important to note that buying shares (called 'going long') has a very different risk profile from _____. In the former case, losses are limited (the price can only go down to zero) but gains are unlimited (there is no limit on how high the price can go.) In short selling, this is reversed, meaning the possible gains are limited (the stock can only go down to a price of zero), and the seller can lose more than the original value of the share, with no upper limit.

a. Naked call
b. Comparative advantage
c. Selling short
d. Cash budget

36. _____ is buying securities with cash borrowed from a broker, using other securities as collateral. This has the effect of magnifying any profit or loss made on the securities. The securities serve as collateral for the loan.

a. Margin buying
b. SPI 200 futures contract
c. Risk-neutral measure
d. Triple witching hour

37. In finance, a _____ is collateral that the holder of a position in securities, options, or futures contracts has to deposit to cover the credit risk of his counterparty (most often his broker.) This risk can arise if the holder has done any of the following:

- borrowed cash from the counterparty to buy securities or options,
- sold securities or options short, or
- entered into a futures contract.

The collateral can be in the form of cash or securities, and it is deposited in a _____ account. On U.S. futures exchanges, '_____' was formally called performance bond.

_____ buying is buying securities with cash borrowed from a broker, using other securities as collateral.

a. Share
b. Procter ' Gamble
c. Credit
d. Margin

38. _____ are those dividends paid out in form of additional stock shares of the issuing corporation or other corporation They are usually issued in proportion to shares owned (for example for every 100 shares of stock owned, 5% stock dividend will yield 5 extra shares). If this payment involves the issue of new shares, this is very similar to a stock split in that it increases the total number of shares while lowering the price of each share and does not change the market capitalization or the total value of the shares held
   a. Time-based currency
   b. Stock or scrip dividends
   c. The Hong Kong Securities Institute
   d. Database auditing

39. A _____ or stock divide increases or decreases the number of shares in a public company. The price is adjusted such that the before and after market capitalization of the company remains the same and dilution does not occur. Options and warrants are included.
   a. Stop order
   b. Contract for difference
   c. Stop price
   d. Stock split

40. _____ is typically a higher ranking stock than voting shares, and its terms are negotiated between the corporation and the investor.

_____ usually carry no voting rights, but may carry superior priority over common stock in the payment of dividends and upon liquidation. _____ may carry a dividend that is paid out prior to any dividends to common stock holders.

a. Follow-on offering
b. Preferred stock
c. Trade-off theory
d. Second lien loan

41. In finance, a _____ is a type of bond that can be converted into shares of stock in the issuing company, usually at some pre-announced ratio. It is a hybrid security with debt- and equity-like features. Although it typically has a low coupon rate, the holder is compensated with the ability to convert the bond to common stock, usually at a substantial discount to the stock's market value.

a. Gilts
b. Corporate bond
c. Convertible bond
d. Bond fund

42. In finance, a _____ is a security that entitles the holder to buy stock of the company that issued it at a specified price, which is usually higher than the stock price at time of issue.

_____s are frequently attached to bonds or preferred stock as a sweetener, allowing the issuer to pay lower interest rates or dividends. They can be used to enhance the yield of the bond, and make them more attractive to potential buyers.

a. Clearing
b. Credit
c. Clearing house
d. Warrant

43. An _____ is a contract written by a seller that conveys to the buyer the right -- but not the obligation -- to buy (in the case of a call _____) or to sell (in the case of a put _____) a particular asset, such as a piece of property such as, among others, a futures contract. In return for granting the _____, the seller collects a payment (the premium) from the buyer.

For example, buying a call _____ provides the right to buy a specified quantity of a security at a set strike price at some time on or before expiration, while buying a put _____ provides the right to sell.

a. Amortization
b. Option
c. AT'T Mobility LLC
d. Annuity

44. A _____ is a financial contract between two parties, the buyer and the seller of this type of option. Often it is simply labeled a 'call'. The buyer of the option has the right, but not the obligation to buy an agreed quantity of a particular commodity or financial instrument (the underlying instrument) from the seller of the option at a certain time (the expiration date) for a certain price (the strike price.)

a. Bear spread
b. Call option
c. Bull spread
d. Bear call spread

45. A _____ is a financial contract between two parties, the seller (writer) and the buyer of the option. The put allows its buyer the right but not the obligation to sell a commodity or financial instrument (the underlying instrument) to the writer (seller) of the option at a certain time for a certain price (the strike price.) The writer (seller) has the obligation to purchase the underlying asset at that strike price, if the buyer exercises the option.

a. Bear call spread
b. Debit spread
c. Bear spread
d. Put option

46. In options, the _____ is a key variable in a derivatives contract between two parties. Where the contract requires delivery of the underlying instrument, the trade will be at the _____, regardless of the spot price (market price) of the underlying instrument at that time.

Definition - The fixed price at which the owner of an option can purchase, in the case of a call in the case of a put, the underlying security or commodity.

a. Naked put
b. Moneyness
c. Strike price
d. Swaption

Chapter 15. Making Your Money Grow: The Stock Market

47. A _____ is a professionally managed type of collective investment scheme that pools money from many investors and invests it in stocks, bonds, short-term money market instruments, and/or other securities. The _____ will have a fund manager that trades the pooled money on a regular basis. Currently, the worldwide value of all _____s totals more than $26 trillion.

Since 1940, there have been three basic types of investment companies in the United States: open-end funds, also known in the US as _____s; unit investment trusts (UITs); and closed-end funds.

   a. Trust company
   b. Financial intermediary
   c. Net asset value
   d. Mutual fund

48. An _____ or index tracker is a collective investment scheme (usually a mutual fund or exchange-traded fund) that aims to replicate the movements of an index of a specific financial market regardless of market conditions.

Tracking can be achieved by trying to hold all of the securities in the index, in the same proportions as the index. Other methods include statistically sampling the market and holding 'representative' securities.

   a. A Random Walk Down Wall Street
   b. AAB
   c. Investment company
   d. Index fund

49. An _____ is an investment vehicle traded on stock exchanges, much like stocks. An ETF holds assets such as stocks or bonds and trades at approximately the same price as the net asset value of its underlying assets over the course of the trading day. Most ETFs track an index, such as the Dow Jones Industrial Average or the S'P 500.
   a. ABN Amro
   b. AAB
   c. A Random Walk Down Wall Street
   d. Exchange-traded fund

50. _____ has become the norm for individual investors and traders over the past decade with many, if not all brokers now offering online services with unique trading platforms.

In the past, investors had to call up their brokers and place an order on the phone. The broker would then enter the order in their system which was linked to trading floors and exchanges.

a. Investment decisions
b. Alternative investment
c. Investing online
d. Asset allocation

Chapter 16. Making Your Money Grow: Real Estate and Other Opportunities

1. _____ involves the purchase, ownership, management, rental and/or sale of real estate for profit. Improvement of realty property as part of a real estate investment strategy is generally considered to be a sub-specialty of _____ called real estate development. Real estate is an asset form with limited liquidity relative to other investments, it is also capital intensive (although capital may be gained through mortgage leverage) and is highly cash flow dependent.
   a. Liquidation value
   b. Tenancy
   c. Real Estate Investment Trust
   d. Real estate investing

2. In finance, a _____ is a debt security, in which the authorized issuer owes the holders a debt and, depending on the terms of the _____, is obliged to pay interest (the coupon) and/or to repay the principal at a later date, termed maturity.

   Thus a _____ is a loan: the issuer is the borrower, the _____ holder is the lender, and the coupon is the interest. _____s provide the borrower with external funds to finance long-term investments, or, in the case of government _____s, to finance current expenditure.

   a. Puttable bond
   b. Catastrophe bonds
   c. Convertible bond
   d. Bond

3. _____, refers to consumption opportunity gained by an entity within a specified time frame, which is generally expressed in monetary terms. However, for households and individuals, '_____ is the sum of all the wages, salaries, profits, interests payments, rents and other forms of earnings received... in a given period of time.' For firms, _____ generally refers to net-profit: what remains of revenue after expenses have been subtracted.
   a. OIBDA
   b. Annual report
   c. Accrual
   d. Income

4. An _____ is a tax levied on the financial income of people, corporations, or other legal entities. Various _____ systems exist, with varying degrees of tax incidence. Income taxation can be progressive, proportional, or regressive.
   a. AAB
   b. A Random Walk Down Wall Street
   c. ABN Amro
   d. Income Tax

Chapter 16. Making Your Money Grow: Real Estate and Other Opportunities 99

5. _____ or financing is to provide capital (funds), which means money for a project, a person, a business or any other private or public institutions.

Those funds can be allocated for either short term or long term purposes. The health fund is a new way of _____ private healthcare centers.

   a. Product life cycle
   b. Proxy fight
   c. Synthetic CDO
   d. Funding

6. In economics, _____ is a measure of the relative satisfaction from or desirability of consumption of various goods and services. Given this measure, one may speak meaningfully of increasing or decreasing _____, and thereby explain economic behavior in terms of attempts to increase one's _____. For illustrative purposes, changes in _____ are sometimes expressed in units called utils.
   a. Utility function
   b. AAB
   c. Utility
   d. A Random Walk Down Wall Street

7. In economics, business, and accounting, a _____ is the value of money that has been used up to produce something, and hence is not available for use anymore. In business, the _____ may be one of acquisition, in which case the amount of money expended to acquire it is counted as _____. In this case, money is the input that is gone in order to acquire the thing.
   a. Sliding scale fees
   b. Marginal cost
   c. Fixed costs
   d. Cost

8. _____ refers to a business or organization attempting to acquire goods or services to accomplish the goals of the enterprise. Though there are several organizations that attempt to set standards in the _____ process, processes can vary greatly between organizations. Typically the word '_____' is not used interchangeably with the word 'procurement', since procurement typically includes Expediting, Supplier Quality, and Traffic and Logistics (T'L) in addition to _____.
   a. 529 plan
   b. 4-4-5 Calendar
   c. 7-Eleven
   d. Purchasing

Chapter 16. Making Your Money Grow: Real Estate and Other Opportunities

9. In finance, _____ occurs when a debtor has not met its legal obligations according to the debt contract, e.g. it has not made a scheduled payment, or has violated a loan covenant (condition) of the debt contract. _____ may occur if the debtor is either unwilling or unable to pay their debt. This can occur with all debt obligations including bonds, mortgages, loans, and promissory notes.
    a. Credit crunch
    b. Debt validation
    c. Vendor finance
    d. Default

10. _____ is a fee paid on borrowed assets. It is the price paid for the use of borrowed money, or, money earned by deposited funds. Assets that are sometimes lent with _____ include money, shares, consumer goods through hire purchase, major assets such as aircraft, and even entire factories in finance lease arrangements.
    a. AAB
    b. Insolvency
    c. A Random Walk Down Wall Street
    d. Interest

11. _____ is the concept of adding accumulated interest back to the principal, so that interest is earned on interest from that moment on. The act of declaring interest to be principal is called compounding (i.e., interest is compounded.) A loan, for example, may have its interest compounded every month: in this case, a loan with $100 principal and 1% interest per month would have a balance of $101 at the end of the first month.
    a. 4-4-5 Calendar
    b. Penny stock
    c. Risk management
    d. Compound interest

12. _____ is a term used in accounting, economics and finance to spread the cost of an asset over the span of several years.

In simple words we can say that _____ is the reduction in the value of an asset due to usage, passage of time, wear and tear, technological outdating or obsolescence, depletion or other such factors.

In accounting, _____ is a term used to describe any method of attributing the historical or purchase cost of an asset across its useful life, roughly corresponding to normal wear and tear.

Chapter 16. Making Your Money Grow: Real Estate and Other Opportunities

a. Bottom line
b. Matching principle
c. Deferred financing costs
d. Depreciation

13. A '_____' is a 'Charge' that is paid to obtain the right to delay a payment. Essentially, the payer purchases the right to make a given payment in the future instead of in the Present. The '_____', or 'Charge' that must be paid to delay the payment, is simply the difference between what the payment amount would be if it were paid in the present and what the payment amount would be paid if it were paid in the future.
   a. Risk modeling
   b. Risk aversion
   c. Discount
   d. Value at risk

14. The _____ is a U.S. government-owned corporation within the Department of Housing and Urban Development

Ginnie Mae provides guarantees on mortgage-backed securities backed by federally insured or guaranteed loans, mainly loans issued by the Federal Housing Administration, Department of Veterans Affairs, Rural Housing Service, and Office of Public and Indian Housing. Ginnie Mae securities are the only MBS that are guaranteed by the United States government.

   a. Certified Emission Reductions
   b. Cash budget
   c. Case-Shiller Home Price Indices
   d. GNMA

15. A _____ is a bond issued by a national government denominated in the country's own currency. Bonds issued by national governments in foreign currencies are normally referred to as sovereign bonds. The first ever _____ was issued by the British government in 1693 to raise money to fund a war against France.
   a. Collateralized debt obligations
   b. Zero-coupon bond
   c. Municipal bond
   d. Government bond

16. A _____ is a form of partnership similar to a general partnership, except that in addition to one or more general partners (GPs), there are one or more limited partners (_____s). It is a partnership in which only one partner is required to be a general partner.

Chapter 16. Making Your Money Grow: Real Estate and Other Opportunities

The GPs are, in all major respects, in the same legal position as partners in a conventional firm, i.e. they have management control, share the right to use partnership property, share the profits of the firm in predefined proportions, and have joint and several liability for the debts of the partnership.

   a. Leverage
   b. Limited partnership
   c. Fund of funds
   d. Limited liability company

17. A _____ is a type of business entity in which partners (owners) share with each other the profits or losses of the business undertaking in which all have invested. _____s are often favored over corporations for taxation purposes, as the _____ structure does not generally incur a tax on profits before it is distributed to the partners (i.e. there is no dividend tax levied.) However, depending on the _____ structure and the jurisdiction in which it operates, owners of a _____ may be exposed to greater personal liability than they would as shareholders of a corporation.
   a. Clayton Antitrust Act
   b. Fiduciary
   c. National Securities Markets Improvement Act of 1996
   d. Partnership

18. _____ provides protection against most risks to property, such as fire, theft and some weather damage. This includes specialized forms of insurance such as fire insurance, flood insurance, earthquake insurance, home insurance or boiler insurance. Property is insured in two main ways - open perils and named perils.
   a. Property insurance
   b. 529 plan
   c. 4-4-5 Calendar
   d. Lenders Mortgage Insurance

19. A _____ is a tax designation for a corporation investing in real estate that reduces or eliminates corporate income taxes. In return, _____s are required to distribute 95% of their income, which may be taxable in the hands of the investors. The _____ structure was designed to provide a similar structure for investment in real estate as mutual funds provide for investment in stocks.
   a. Liquidation value
   b. Real estate investing
   c. Real Estate Investment Trust
   d. REIT

Chapter 16. Making Your Money Grow: Real Estate and Other Opportunities

20. A _____ or _____ is a tax designation for a corporation investing in real estate that reduces or eliminates corporate income taxes. In return, _____s are required to distribute 95% of their income, which may be taxable in the hands of the investors. The _____ structure was designed to provide a similar structure for investment in real estate as mutual funds provide for investment in stocks.

   a. Real estate investment trust
   b. Liquidation value
   c. Tenancy
   d. Real estate investing

21. A _____ is a bond issued by a corporation. The term is usually applied to longer-term debt instruments, generally with a maturity date falling at least a year after their issue date. (The term 'commercial paper' is sometimes used for instruments with a shorter maturity.)

   a. Brady bonds
   b. Government bond
   c. Serial bond
   d. Corporate bond

22. In finance, the _____ is the global financial market for short-term borrowing and lending. It provides short-term liquidity funding for the global financial system. The _____ is where short-term obligations such as Treasury bills, commercial paper and bankers' acceptances are bought and sold.

   a. Debt-for-equity swap
   b. Consumer debt
   c. Cramdown
   d. Money market

23. A _____ is a private or public market for the trading of company stock and derivatives of company stock at an agreed price; these are securities listed on a stock exchange as well as those only traded privately.

The size of the world _____ is estimated at about $36.6 trillion US at the beginning of October 2008. The world derivatives market has been estimated at about $480 trillion face or nominal value, 12 times the size of the entire world economy.

   a. Anton Gelonkin
   b. Andrew Tobias
   c. Adolph Coors
   d. Stock market

Chapter 16. Making Your Money Grow: Real Estate and Other Opportunities

24. In the original and simplified sense, _____ were things of value, of uniform quality, that were produced in large quantities by many different producers; the items from each different producer are considered equivalent. It is the contract and this underlying standard that define the commodity, not any quality inherent in the product.

_____ exchanges include:

- Chicago Board of Trade
- Kansas City Board of Trade
- Euronext.liffe
- Kuala Lumpur Futures Exchange
- Bhatinda Om ' Oil Exchange
- London Metal Exchange
- New York Mercantile Exchange
- Multi Commodity Exchange
- Dalian Commodity Exchange

Markets for trading _____ can be very efficient, particularly if the division into pools matches demand segments. These markets will quickly respond to changes in supply and demand to find an equilibrium price and quantity.

a. Commodities
b. 4-4-5 Calendar
c. 7-Eleven
d. 529 plan

25. _____ (in a financial context) is the assumption of the risk of loss, in return for the uncertain possibility of a reward. Only if one may safely say that a particular position involves no risk may one say, strictly speaking, that such a position represents an 'investment.' Financial _____ involves the buying, holding, selling, and short-selling of stocks, bonds, commodities, currencies, collectibles, real estate, derivatives, or any valuable financial instrument to profit from fluctuations in its price as opposed to buying it for use or for income via methods such as dividends or interest. _____ represents one of four market roles in Western financial markets, distinct from hedging, long- or short-term investing, and arbitrage.

a. Forward market
b. Market anomaly
c. Central Securities Depository
d. Speculation

26. A _____ is something for which there is demand, but which is supplied without qualitative differentiation across a market. It is a product that is the same no matter who produces it, such as petroleum, notebook paper, or milk. In other words, copper is copper.

Chapter 16. Making Your Money Grow: Real Estate and Other Opportunities

a. 7-Eleven
b. 4-4-5 Calendar
c. 529 plan
d. Commodity

27. An _____ represents the ownership in the shares of a foreign company trading on US financial markets. The stock of many non-US companies trades on US exchanges through the use of _____s. _____s enable US investors to buy shares in foreign companies without undertaking cross-border transactions.

a. ABN Amro
b. AAB
c. A Random Walk Down Wall Street
d. American depository receipt

28. The term _____ or economic cycle refers to the fluctuations of economic activity (business fluctuations) around a long-term growth trend. The cycle involves shifts over time between periods of relatively rapid growth of output (recovery and prosperity), and periods of relative stagnation or decline (contraction or recession.) These fluctuations are often measured using the real gross domestic product.

a. Fixed exchange rate
b. Deflation
c. Behavioral finance
d. Business cycle

29. A _____ is a professionally managed type of collective investment scheme that pools money from many investors and invests it in stocks, bonds, short-term money market instruments, and/or other securities. The _____ will have a fund manager that trades the pooled money on a regular basis. Currently, the worldwide value of all _____s totals more than $26 trillion.

Since 1940, there have been three basic types of investment companies in the United States: open-end funds, also known in the US as _____s; unit investment trusts (UITs); and closed-end funds.

a. Trust company
b. Financial intermediary
c. Net asset value
d. Mutual fund

Chapter 16. Making Your Money Grow: Real Estate and Other Opportunities

30. A _____ is a rare metallic chemical element of high economic value. Chemically, the _____s are less reactive than most elements, have high luster, are softer or more ductile, and have higher melting points than other metals. Historically, _____s were important as currency, but are now regarded mainly as investment and industrial commodities.

   a. 7-Eleven
   b. Precious metal
   c. 529 plan
   d. 4-4-5 Calendar

31. _____ is a political organization established in 2002 and dedicated to the protection of children from abuse, exploitation and neglect. It is a nonprofit, 501(c)(4) membership association with members in every U.S. state and 10 nations. _____ achieved great success in its first three years, winning legislative victories in eight state legislatures.

   a. Ford Foundation
   b. First Prudential Markets
   c. The Depository Trust ' Clearing Corporation
   d. Protect

32. In business and finance, a _____ (also referred to as equity _____) of stock means a _____ of ownership in a corporation (company.) In the plural, stocks is often used as a synonym for _____s especially in the United States, but it is less commonly used that way outside of North America.

   In the United Kingdom, South Africa, and Australia, stock can also refer to completely different financial instruments such as government bonds or, less commonly, to all kinds of marketable securities.

   a. Share
   b. Bucket shop
   c. Procter ' Gamble
   d. Margin

Chapter 17. Life, Health, and Income Insurance

1. In financial accounting, the term _____ is most commonly used to describe any part of shareholders' equity, except for basic share capital. Sometimes, the term is used instead of the term provision; such a use, however, is inconsistent with the terminology suggested by International Accounting Standards Board. For more information about provisions, see provision (accounting.)

   a. Reserve
   b. Treasury stock
   c. Closing entries
   d. FIFO and LIFO accounting

2. _____ is the provision of resources (such as granting a loan) by one party to another party where that second party does not reimburse the first party immediately, thereby generating a debt, and instead arranges either to repay or return those resources (or material(s) of equal value) at a later date. The first party is called a creditor, also known as a lender, while the second party is called a debtor, also known as a borrower.

   Movements of financial capital are normally dependent on either _____ or equity transfers.

   a. Clearing house
   b. Comparable
   c. Warrant
   d. Credit

3. Credit insurance is a term used to describe both trade credit insurance and _____.

   _____ is a consumer purchase, often sold with a big ticket purchase such as an automobile. The insurance will pay off the loan balance in the event of the death or the disability of the borrower.

   a. 529 plan
   b. 7-Eleven
   c. 4-4-5 Calendar
   d. Credit life insurance

4. _____ is a form of life insurance such as whole life or endowment, where the policy is for the life of the insured, the payout is assured at the end of the policy (assuming the policy is kept current) and the policy accrues cash value.

   This is compared with Term life insurance where insurance is purchased for a specified period (typically a year, or for level periods such as 5, 10, 15, 20 even 25 and 30 years) where a death benefit is only paid to the beneficiary if the insured dies during the specified period.

   _____ originally was offered as a fixed premium fixed return product known as whole life insurance also known as cash surrender life insurance.

a. 4-4-5 Calendar
b. Whole life insurance
c. 529 plan
d. Permanent life insurance

5. _____ is a life insurance policy that remains in force for the insured's whole life and requires (in most cases) premiums to be paid every year into the policy.

All life insurance was originally term insurance. However, because term life insurance only pays a claim upon death within the stated term, most term insurance policy holders became upset over the idea that they could be paying premiums for 20 or 30 years and then wind up with nothing to show for it.

a. Term life insurance
b. 4-4-5 Calendar
c. 529 plan
d. Whole life insurance

6. The phrase _____ refers to the aspect of corporate strategy, corporate finance and management dealing with the buying, selling and combining of different companies that can aid, finance, or help a growing company in a given industry grow rapidly without having to create another business entity.

An acquisition, also known as a takeover, is the buying of one company (the 'target') by another. An acquisition may be friendly or hostile.

a. 529 plan
b. 4-4-5 Calendar
c. 7-Eleven
d. Mergers and acquisitions

7. _____ or term assurance is life insurance which provides coverage for a limited period of time, the relevant term. After that period, the insured can either drop the policy or pay annually increasing premiums to continue the coverage. If the insured dies during the term, the death benefit will be paid to the beneficiary.

a. Whole life insurance
b. Term life insurance
c. 529 plan
d. 4-4-5 Calendar

Chapter 17. Life, Health, and Income Insurance

8. _____ is a type of permanent life insurance based on a cash value. That is, the policy is established with the insurer where premium payments above the cost of insurance are credited to the cash value. The cash value is credited each month with interest, and the policy is debited each month by a cost of insurance (COI) charge, and any other policy charges and fees which are drawn from the cash value if no premium payment is made that month.
   a. Universal life
   b. ABN Amro
   c. A Random Walk Down Wall Street
   d. AAB

9. A _____ is an exchange of promises between two or more parties to do an act which is enforceable in a court of law. It is where an unqualified offer meets a qualified acceptance and the parties reach Consensus ad Idem. The parties must have the necessary capacity to _____ and the _____ must not be either trifling, indeterminate, impossible or illegal.
   a. 7-Eleven
   b. 4-4-5 Calendar
   c. Contract
   d. 529 plan

10. An _____ is a sum paid by A to B by way of compensation for a particular loss suffered by B. The indemnifying party (A) may or may not be responsible for the loss suffered by the indemnified party (B.) Forms of _____ include cash payments, repairs, replacement, and reinstatement.

    In common parlance, _____ is often used as a synonym for compensation or reparation.

    a. Indemnity
    b. AAB
    c. A Random Walk Down Wall Street
    d. ABN Amro

11. A _____ is a payment made by a corporation to its shareholder members. When a corporation earns a profit or surplus, that money can be put to two uses: it can either be re-invested in the business (called retained earnings), or it can be paid to the shareholders as a _____. Many corporations retain a portion of their earnings and pay the remainder as a _____.
    a. Dividend
    b. Dividend puzzle
    c. Dividend yield
    d. Special dividend

Chapter 17. Life, Health, and Income Insurance

12. An _____ is a contract written by a seller that conveys to the buyer the right -- but not the obligation -- to buy (in the case of a call _____) or to sell (in the case of a put _____) a particular asset, such as a piece of property such as, among others, a futures contract. In return for granting the _____, the seller collects a payment (the premium) from the buyer.

For example, buying a call _____ provides the right to buy a specified quantity of a security at a set strike price at some time on or before expiration, while buying a put _____ provides the right to sell.

    a. AT'T Mobility LLC
    b. Option
    c. Annuity
    d. Amortization

13. Unemployment occurs when a person is available to work and currently seeking work, but the person is without work. The prevalence of unemployment is usually measured using the _____, which is defined as the percentage of those in the labor force who are unemployed. The _____ is also used in economic studies and economic indexes such as the United States' Conference Board's Index of Leading Indicators as a measure of the state of the macroeconomics.

    a. ABN Amro
    b. A Random Walk Down Wall Street
    c. AAB
    d. Unemployment rate

14. In economics, business, and accounting, a _____ is the value of money that has been used up to produce something, and hence is not available for use anymore. In business, the _____ may be one of acquisition, in which case the amount of money expended to acquire it is counted as _____. In this case, money is the input that is gone in order to acquire the thing.

    a. Cost
    b. Sliding scale fees
    c. Fixed costs
    d. Marginal cost

15. _____, in bookkeeping, refers to assets, liabilities, income, and expenses recorded on individual pages of the so called book of final entry or ledger. Changes in _____ value are made by chronologically posting debit (DR) and credit (CR) entries to its page. Examples of _____s are cash, _____s receivable, mortgages, loans, land and buildings, common stock, sales, services provided, wages, and payroll overhead.

Chapter 17. Life, Health, and Income Insurance

a. Accretion
b. Option
c. Alpha
d. Account

16. In health insurance in the United States, a _____ is a managed care organization of medical doctors, hospitals, and other health care providers who have covenanted with an insurer or a third-party administrator to provide health care at reduced rates to the insurer's or administrator's clients.

A _____ is a subscription-based medical care arrangement. A membership allows a substantial discount below their regularly-charged rates from the designated professionals partnered with the organization.

a. Preferred provider organization
b. Title insurance
c. 529 plan
d. 4-4-5 Calendar

17. A _____ is a fungible, negotiable instrument representing financial value. They are broadly categorized into debt securities (such as banknotes, bonds and debentures), and equity securities; e.g., common stocks. The company or other entity issuing the _____ is called the issuer.
a. Security
b. Tracking stock
c. Book entry
d. Securities lending

18. _____, refers to consumption opportunity gained by an entity within a specified time frame, which is generally expressed in monetary terms. However, for households and individuals, '_____ is the sum of all the wages, salaries, profits, interests payments, rents and other forms of earnings received... in a given period of time.' For firms, _____ generally refers to net-profit: what remains of revenue after expenses have been subtracted.
a. Income
b. Annual report
c. OIBDA
d. Accrual

19. An _____ is a tax levied on the financial income of people, corporations, or other legal entities. Various _____ systems exist, with varying degrees of tax incidence. Income taxation can be progressive, proportional, or regressive.

a. Income tax
b. A Random Walk Down Wall Street
c. ABN Amro
d. AAB

Chapter 18. Financial Planning for Later Years 113

1. _____, in a financial context, refers to the allocation of finances for retirement. This normally means the setting aside of money or other assets to obtain a steady income at retirement. The goal of _____ is to achieve financial independence, so that the need to be gainfully employed is optional rather than a necessity.
   a. 7-Eleven
   b. 529 plan
   c. Retirement planning
   d. 4-4-5 Calendar

2. _____ refers to the replacement of an existing debt obligation with a debt obligation bearing different terms. The most common consumer _____ is for a home mortgage.

   _____ may be undertaken to reduce interest rate/interest costs (by _____ at a lower rate), to extend the repayment time, to pay off other debt(s), to reduce one's periodic payment obligations (sometimes by taking a longer-term loan), to reduce or alter risk (such as by _____ from a variable-rate to a fixed-rate loan), and/or to raise cash for investment, consumption, or the payment of a dividend.

   a. 4-4-5 Calendar
   b. Refinancing
   c. 529 plan
   d. 7-Eleven

3. A _____ is a bond issued by a corporation. The term is usually applied to longer-term debt instruments, generally with a maturity date falling at least a year after their issue date. (The term 'commercial paper' is sometimes used for instruments with a shorter maturity.)
   a. Government bond
   b. Brady bonds
   c. Serial bond
   d. Corporate bond

4. In finance, the _____ is the global financial market for short-term borrowing and lending. It provides short-term liquidity funding for the global financial system. The _____ is where short-term obligations such as Treasury bills, commercial paper and bankers' acceptances are bought and sold.
   a. Cramdown
   b. Consumer debt
   c. Debt-for-equity swap
   d. Money market

Chapter 18. Financial Planning for Later Years

5. _____ involves the purchase, ownership, management, rental and/or sale of real estate for profit. Improvement of realty property as part of a real estate investment strategy is generally considered to be a sub-specialty of _____ called real estate development. Real estate is an asset form with limited liquidity relative to other investments, it is also capital intensive (although capital may be gained through mortgage leverage) and is highly cash flow dependent.

   a. Tenancy
   b. Real estate investing
   c. Real Estate Investment Trust
   d. Liquidation value

6. A _____ is a private or public market for the trading of company stock and derivatives of company stock at an agreed price; these are securities listed on a stock exchange as well as those only traded privately.

   The size of the world _____ is estimated at about $36.6 trillion US at the beginning of October 2008. The world derivatives market has been estimated at about $480 trillion face or nominal value, 12 times the size of the entire world economy.

   a. Andrew Tobias
   b. Anton Gelonkin
   c. Stock market
   d. Adolph Coors

7. In finance, a _____ is a debt security, in which the authorized issuer owes the holders a debt and, depending on the terms of the _____, is obliged to pay interest (the coupon) and/or to repay the principal at a later date, termed maturity.

   Thus a _____ is a loan: the issuer is the borrower, the _____ holder is the lender, and the coupon is the interest. _____s provide the borrower with external funds to finance long-term investments, or, in the case of government _____s, to finance current expenditure.

   a. Bond
   b. Puttable bond
   c. Convertible bond
   d. Catastrophe bonds

8. In economics, _____ is a rise in the general level of prices of goods and services in an economy over a period of time. The term '_____' once referred to increases in the money supply (monetary _____); however, economic debates about the relationship between money supply and price levels have led to its primary use today in describing price _____. _____ can also be described as a decline in the real value of money--a loss of purchasing power in the medium of exchange which is also the monetary unit of account.

Chapter 18. Financial Planning for Later Years 115

a. ABN Amro
b. Inflation
c. AAB
d. A Random Walk Down Wall Street

9. The _____ of 1974 (Pub.L. 93-406, 88 Stat. 829, enacted September 2, 1974) is an American federal statute that establishes minimum standards for pension plans in private industry and provides for extensive rules on the federal income tax effects of transactions associated with employee benefit plans.
   a. Expedited Funds Availability Act
   b. Articles of Partnership
   c. Express warranty
   d. Employee Retirement Income Security Act

10. A _____ is a fungible, negotiable instrument representing financial value. They are broadly categorized into debt securities (such as banknotes, bonds and debentures), and equity securities; e.g., common stocks. The company or other entity issuing the _____ is called the issuer.
    a. Tracking stock
    b. Security
    c. Book entry
    d. Securities lending

11. _____ is commonly defined as the amount of a company's or a person's income before all deductions or any taxpayer's income, except that which is specifically excluded by the Internal Revenue Code, before taking deductions or taxes into account. For a business, this amount is pre-tax net sales less cost of sales. Section 61 of the Internal Revenue Code (Code) defines '_____' as 'all income from whatever source derived.' Section 61(a) of the Code lists fifteen examples of items included in _____; however, the list is not exhaustive.
    a. Second lien loan
    b. Financial distress
    c. Gross income
    d. Shareholder value

12. _____, refers to consumption opportunity gained by an entity within a specified time frame, which is generally expressed in monetary terms. However, for households and individuals, '_____ is the sum of all the wages, salaries, profits, interests payments, rents and other forms of earnings received... in a given period of time.' For firms, _____ generally refers to net-profit: what remains of revenue after expenses have been subtracted.

a. OIBDA
b. Annual report
c. Accrual
d. Income

13. _____ is the value of a homeowner's unencumbered interest in their property, i.e. the difference between the home's fair market value and the unpaid balance of the mortgage and any outstanding debt over the home. _____ increases as the mortgage is paid or as the property enjoys appreciation. This is sometimes called real property value in economics.
   a. Liquidation value
   b. Home equity
   c. REIT
   d. Real Estate Investment Trust

14. _____s are full-fledged pension plans for self-employed people in the United States. They are sometimes called HR10 plans and are not Individual Retirement Accounts (IRA.)

Since a _____ is a full-fledged pension, there is a Keogh for every employer-sponsored pension-plan design.

   a. 529 plan
   b. 4-4-5 Calendar
   c. 7-Eleven
   d. Keogh plan

15. The term _____ or economic cycle refers to the fluctuations of economic activity (business fluctuations) around a long-term growth trend. The cycle involves shifts over time between periods of relatively rapid growth of output (recovery and prosperity), and periods of relative stagnation or decline (contraction or recession.) These fluctuations are often measured using the real gross domestic product.
   a. Deflation
   b. Behavioral finance
   c. Business cycle
   d. Fixed exchange rate

16. A _____ is a pool of assets forming an independent legal entity that are bought with the contributions to a pension plan for the exclusive purpose of financing pension plan benefits.

Chapter 18. Financial Planning for Later Years 117

_____s are important shareholders of listed and private companies. They are especially important to the stock market where large institutional investors like the Ontario Teachers' Pension Plan dominate.

a. Leverage
b. Limited liability company
c. Leveraged buyout
d. Pension fund

17. In law, _____ is to give an immediately secured right of present or future enjoyment. One has a vested right to an asset that cannot be taken away by any third party, even though one may not yet possess the asset. When the right, interest or title to the present or future possession of a legal estate can be transferred to any other party, it is termed a vested interest.

a. Limited liability
b. Competition law
c. Corporate governance
d. Vesting

18. _____ or financing is to provide capital (funds), which means money for a project, a person, a business or any other private or public institutions.

Those funds can be allocated for either short term or long term purposes. The health fund is a new way of _____ private healthcare centers.

a. Funding
b. Product life cycle
c. Proxy fight
d. Synthetic CDO

19. The institution most often referenced by the word '_____' is a public or publicly traded _____, the shares of which are traded on a public stock exchange (e.g., the New York Stock Exchange or Nasdaq in the United States) where shares of stock of _____s are bought and sold by and to the general public. Most of the largest businesses in the world are publicly traded _____s. However, the majority of _____s are said to be closely held, privately held or close _____s, meaning that no ready market exists for the trading of shares.

a. Protect
b. Federal Home Loan Mortgage Corporation
c. Depository Trust Company
d. Corporation

Chapter 18. Financial Plannina for Later Years

20. An _____ is a retirement plan account that provides some tax advantages for retirement savings in the United States.
   a. A Random Walk Down Wall Street
   b. AAB
   c. ABN Amro
   d. Individual Retirement Arrangement

21. _____, in bookkeeping, refers to assets, liabilities, income, and expenses recorded on individual pages of the so called book of final entry or ledger. Changes in _____ value are made by chronologically posting debit (DR) and credit (CR) entries to its page. Examples of _____s are cash, _____s receivable, mortgages, loans, land and buildings, common stock, sales, services provided, wages, and payroll overhead.
   a. Option
   b. Accretion
   c. Alpha
   d. Account

22. In economics, business, and accounting, a _____ is the value of money that has been used up to produce something, and hence is not available for use anymore. In business, the _____ may be one of acquisition, in which case the amount of money expended to acquire it is counted as _____. In this case, money is the input that is gone in order to acquire the thing.
   a. Fixed costs
   b. Marginal cost
   c. Cost
   d. Sliding scale fees

Chapter 19. Estate Planning

1. _____ is the process of disposing of an estate. _____ typically attempts to eliminate uncertainties over the administration of a probate and maximize the value of the estate by reducing taxes and other expenses. Guardians are often designated for minor children and beneficiaries in incapacity.
    a. AAB
    b. A Random Walk Down Wall Street
    c. ABN Amro
    d. Estate planning

2. In finance, a _____ is a debt security, in which the authorized issuer owes the holders a debt and, depending on the terms of the _____, is obliged to pay interest (the coupon) and/or to repay the principal at a later date, termed maturity.

    Thus a _____ is a loan: the issuer is the borrower, the _____ holder is the lender, and the coupon is the interest. _____s provide the borrower with external funds to finance long-term investments, or, in the case of government _____s, to finance current expenditure.

    a. Convertible bond
    b. Catastrophe bonds
    c. Puttable bond
    d. Bond

3. _____ is the legal process of administering the estate of a deceased person by resolving all claims and distributing the deceased person's property under the valid will. A surrogate court decides the validity of a testator's will. A _____ interprets the instructions of the deceased, decides the executor as the personal representative of the estate, and adjudicates the interests of heirs and other parties who may have claims against the estate.
    a. 4-4-5 Calendar
    b. 7-Eleven
    c. Probate
    d. 529 plan

4. _____ is that which is owed; usually referencing assets owed, but the term can cover other obligations. In the case of assets, _____ is a means of using future purchasing power in the present before a summation has been earned. Some companies and corporations use _____ as a part of their overall corporate finance strategy.
    a. Credit cycle
    b. Partial Payment
    c. Cross-collateralization
    d. Debt

Chapter 19. Estate Planning

5. An _____ is a contract written by a seller that conveys to the buyer the right -- but not the obligation -- to buy (in the case of a call _____) or to sell (in the case of a put _____) a particular asset, such as a piece of property such as, among others, a futures contract. In return for granting the _____, the seller collects a payment (the premium) from the buyer.

For example, buying a call _____ provides the right to buy a specified quantity of a security at a set strike price at some time on or before expiration, while buying a put _____ provides the right to sell.

    a. Annuity
    b. AT'T Mobility LLC
    c. Amortization
    d. Option

6. _____ is a measure of the ability of a debtor to pay their debts as and when they fall due. It is usually expressed as a ratio or a percentage of current liabilities.

For a corporation with a published balance sheet there are various ratios used to calculate a measure of liquidity.

    a. Operating profit margin
    b. Accounting liquidity
    c. Invested capital
    d. Operating leverage

7. In business and accounting, _____s are everything of value that is owned by a person or company. The balance sheet of a firm records the monetary value of the _____s owned by the firm. The two major _____ classes are tangible _____s and intangible _____s.

    a. Accounts payable
    b. EBITDA
    c. Asset
    d. Income

8. _____, refers to consumption opportunity gained by an entity within a specified time frame, which is generally expressed in monetary terms. However, for households and individuals, '_____ is the sum of all the wages, salaries, profits, interests payments, rents and other forms of earnings received... in a given period of time.' For firms, _____ generally refers to net-profit: what remains of revenue after expenses have been subtracted.

a. Accrual
b. Annual report
c. Income
d. OIBDA

9. An _____ is a tax levied on the financial income of people, corporations, or other legal entities. Various _____ systems exist, with varying degrees of tax incidence. Income taxation can be progressive, proportional, or regressive.
   a. ABN Amro
   b. AAB
   c. A Random Walk Down Wall Street
   d. Income tax

Chapter 20. Income Taxes

1. _____, refers to consumption opportunity gained by an entity within a specified time frame, which is generally expressed in monetary terms. However, for households and individuals, '_____ is the sum of all the wages, salaries, profits, interests payments, rents and other forms of earnings received... in a given period of time.' For firms, _____ generally refers to net-profit: what remains of revenue after expenses have been subtracted.
   a. Annual report
   b. Accrual
   c. OIBDA
   d. Income

2. An _____ is a tax levied on the financial income of people, corporations, or other legal entities. Various _____ systems exist, with varying degrees of tax incidence. Income taxation can be progressive, proportional, or regressive.
   a. A Random Walk Down Wall Street
   b. Income tax
   c. ABN Amro
   d. AAB

3. _____ is commonly defined as the amount of a company's or a person's income before all deductions or any taxpayer's income, except that which is specifically excluded by the Internal Revenue Code, before taking deductions or taxes into account. For a business, this amount is pre-tax net sales less cost of sales. Section 61 of the Internal Revenue Code (Code) defines '_____' as 'all income from whatever source derived.' Section 61(a) of the Code lists fifteen examples of items included in _____; however, the list is not exhaustive.
   a. Gross income
   b. Financial distress
   c. Shareholder value
   d. Second lien loan

4. A _____ is a payment made by a corporation to its shareholder members. When a corporation earns a profit or surplus, that money can be put to two uses: it can either be re-invested in the business (called retained earnings), or it can be paid to the shareholders as a _____. Many corporations retain a portion of their earnings and pay the remainder as a _____.
   a. Dividend puzzle
   b. Dividend
   c. Dividend yield
   d. Special dividend

5. _____ is a fee paid on borrowed assets. It is the price paid for the use of borrowed money , or, money earned by deposited funds . Assets that are sometimes lent with _____ include money, shares, consumer goods through hire purchase, major assets such as aircraft, and even entire factories in finance lease arrangements.

Chapter 20. Income Taxes

a. Insolvency
b. AAB
c. A Random Walk Down Wall Street
d. Interest

6. _____ are the inflation-indexed bonds issued by the U.S. Treasury. The principal is adjusted to the Consumer Price Index, the commonly used measure of inflation. The coupon rate is constant, but generates a different amount of interest when multiplied by the inflation-adjusted principal, thus protecting the holder against inflation. _____ are currently offered in 5-year, 10-year and 20-year maturities.
   a. 4-4-5 Calendar
   b. Treasury Inflation-Protected Securities
   c. Treasury securities
   d. Treasury Inflation Protected Securities

7. _____ is the portion of income that is the subject of taxation according to the laws that determine what is income and the taxation rate for that income. Generally, _____ refers to an individual's (or corporation's) gross income, adjusted for various deductions allowable by statute. The main questions put by most individuals in any jurisdiction are 'what makes up my _____' and what tax rates should be applied such that I can work out my tax liability to the state.
   a. Taxable Income
   b. 529 plan
   c. 4-4-5 Calendar
   d. 7-Eleven

8. The term _____ or economic cycle refers to the fluctuations of economic activity (business fluctuations) around a long-term growth trend. The cycle involves shifts over time between periods of relatively rapid growth of output (recovery and prosperity), and periods of relative stagnation or decline (contraction or recession.) These fluctuations are often measured using the real gross domestic product.
   a. Deflation
   b. Business cycle
   c. Fixed exchange rate
   d. Behavioral finance

9. _____ means regulating, adapting or settling in a variety of contexts:

In commercial law, _____ means the settlement of a loss incurred on insured goods. The calculation of the amounts of compensation to be paid by or to the several interests is a complicated matter. It involves much detail and arithmetic, and requires a full and accurate knowledge of the principles of the subject.

a. Asset recovery
b. Intelligent investor
c. Equity method
d. Adjustment

10. _____ is the provision of resources (such as granting a loan) by one party to another party where that second party does not reimburse the first party immediately, thereby generating a debt, and instead arranges either to repay or return those resources (or material(s) of equal value) at a later date. The first party is called a creditor, also known as a lender, while the second party is called a debtor, also known as a borrower.

Movements of financial capital are normally dependent on either _____ or equity transfers.

a. Comparable
b. Credit
c. Clearing house
d. Warrant

11. _____ generally refers to two kinds of taxes: Taxes which employers are required to withhold from employees' pay Pay-As-You-Earn or Pay-As-You-Go tax; and taxes which are paid from the employer's own funds and which are directly related to employing a worker, which may be either fixed charges or proportionally linked to an employee's pay.

In China, the _____ is a specific tax which is paid to states and territories by employers, not by employees. The tax is not deducted from the worker's pay.

a. Tax brackets
b. Capital gain
c. Withholding tax
d. Payroll tax

Chapter 21. Working for Yourself

1. An _____ is a natural person, business, or corporation which provides goods or services to another entity under terms specified in a contract or within a verbal agreement. Unlike an employee, an _____ does not work regularly for an employer but works as and when required, during which time she or he may be subject to the Law of Agency. _____s are usually paid on a freelance basis.
   a. Independent contractor
   b. ABN Amro
   c. A Random Walk Down Wall Street
   d. AAB

2. A sole _____, or simply _____ is a type of business entity which legally has no separate existence from its owner. Hence, the limitations of liability enjoyed by a corporation and limited liability partnerships do not apply to sole proprietors. All debts of the business are debts of the owner.
   a. Product life cycle
   b. Just-in-time
   c. Free cash flow
   d. Proprietorship

3. The institution most often referenced by the word '_____' is a public or publicly traded _____, the shares of which are traded on a public stock exchange (e.g., the New York Stock Exchange or Nasdaq in the United States) where shares of stock of _____s are bought and sold by and to the general public. Most of the largest businesses in the world are publicly traded _____s. However, the majority of _____s are said to be closely held, privately held or close _____s, meaning that no ready market exists for the trading of shares.
   a. Federal Home Loan Mortgage Corporation
   b. Depository Trust Company
   c. Corporation
   d. Protect

4. _____s are full-fledged pension plans for self-employed people in the United States. They are sometimes called HR10 plans and are not Individual Retirement Accounts (IRA.)

   Since a _____ is a full-fledged pension, there is a Keogh for every employer-sponsored pension-plan design.

   a. 4-4-5 Calendar
   b. 529 plan
   c. Keogh plan
   d. 7-Eleven

5. A _____ is a type of business entity in which partners (owners) share with each other the profits or losses of the business undertaking in which all have invested. _____s are often favored over corporations for taxation purposes, as the _____ structure does not generally incur a tax on profits before it is distributed to the partners (i.e. there is no dividend tax levied.) However, depending on the _____ structure and the jurisdiction in which it operates, owners of a _____ may be exposed to greater personal liability than they would as shareholders of a corporation.

   a. National Securities Markets Improvement Act of 1996
   b. Fiduciary
   c. Clayton Antitrust Act
   d. Partnership

6. _____ is a process by which a firm can obtain the use of a certain fixed assets for which it must pay a series of contractual, periodic, tax deductible payments. The lessee is the receiver of the services or the assets under the lease contract and the lessor is the owner of the assets. The relationship between the tenant and the landlord is called a tenancy, and can be for a fixed or an indefinite period of time (called the term of the lease).

   a. Royalties
   b. Leasing
   c. Quiet period
   d. Foreign Corrupt Practices Act

7. A _____ is an exchange of promises between two or more parties to do an act which is enforceable in a court of law. It is where an unqualified offer meets a qualified acceptance and the parties reach Consensus ad Idem. The parties must have the necessary capacity to _____ and the _____ must not be either trifling, indeterminate, impossible or illegal.

   a. 4-4-5 Calendar
   b. 529 plan
   c. 7-Eleven
   d. Contract

8. _____ or financing is to provide capital (funds), which means money for a project, a person, a business or any other private or public institutions.

   Those funds can be allocated for either short term or long term purposes. The health fund is a new way of _____ private healthcare centers.

   a. Proxy fight
   b. Product life cycle
   c. Funding
   d. Synthetic CDO

Chapter 21. Working for Yourself

9. _____, refers to consumption opportunity gained by an entity within a specified time frame, which is generally expressed in monetary terms. However, for households and individuals, '_____ is the sum of all the wages, salaries, profits, interests payments, rents and other forms of earnings received... in a given period of time.' For firms, _____ generally refers to net-profit: what remains of revenue after expenses have been subtracted.
   a. OIBDA
   b. Accrual
   c. Annual report
   d. Income

10. An _____ is a tax levied on the financial income of people, corporations, or other legal entities. Various _____ systems exist, with varying degrees of tax incidence. Income taxation can be progressive, proportional, or regressive.
    a. AAB
    b. ABN Amro
    c. A Random Walk Down Wall Street
    d. Income tax

11. _____ is that which is owed; usually referencing assets owed, but the term can cover other obligations. In the case of assets, _____ is a means of using future purchasing power in the present before a summation has been earned. Some companies and corporations use _____ as a part of their overall corporate finance strategy.
    a. Cross-collateralization
    b. Debt
    c. Credit cycle
    d. Partial Payment

ANSWER KEY

Chapter 1
1. c 2. d 3. c 4. c 5. b 6. d 7. b 8. d 9. d 10. b
11. d 12. d 13. d 14. d

Chapter 2
1. d 2. d 3. d 4. d 5. c 6. a 7. d 8. d 9. a 10. a
11. b 12. b 13. d 14. d 15. c 16. d 17. b 18. b 19. d 20. d
21. b 22. b 23. a 24. d 25. d 26. d 27. d 28. d

Chapter 3
1. d 2. d 3. b 4. b 5. d 6. d 7. d 8. c 9. d

Chapter 4
1. b 2. a 3. d 4. a 5. a 6. b 7. d 8. d 9. c 10. c
11. b 12. b

Chapter 5
1. d 2. d 3. d 4. c 5. a 6. b 7. c 8. c 9. d 10. d
11. d 12. b

Chapter 6
1. a 2. d 3. d 4. d 5. c 6. a 7. d 8. c 9. a 10. c
11. d 12. b 13. c 14. a 15. c 16. d 17. d 18. a

Chapter 7
1. b 2. a 3. c 4. d 5. b 6. d 7. b 8. b 9. d 10. d
11. d 12. d 13. d 14. a 15. c 16. d 17. a 18. c 19. b 20. c
21. b 22. b 23. c 24. c 25. d 26. d 27. d 28. a

Chapter 8
1. a 2. d 3. b 4. b 5. a 6. d 7. b 8. b 9. d 10. d
11. c 12. b 13. c 14. d

Chapter 9
1. a 2. a 3. d 4. d 5. d 6. c 7. c 8. d 9. a 10. c
11. d 12. d

Chapter 10
1. d 2. b 3. d 4. a 5. d 6. c 7. c

Chapter 11
1. a 2. c 3. b 4. d 5. d 6. d 7. d 8. a 9. c 10. c
11. c 12. d 13. c 14. b 15. d 16. d 17. b 18. d 19. d 20. a
21. d 22. d 23. c

ANSWER KEY

Chapter 12
1. a   2. a   3. a   4. b   5. d   6. d   7. b   8. d   9. d   10. d
11. b 12. d 13. a 14. c 15. d 16. b 17. d 18. d 19. c 20. a
21. d 22. a 23. d 24. c

Chapter 13
1. b   2. d   3. a   4. d   5. b   6. c   7. d   8. d   9. d   10. d
11. d 12. a 13. c 14. d 15. d 16. d 17. a 18. d 19. d 20. d
21. d 22. a 23. d 24. b 25. d 26. a

Chapter 14
1. d   2. d   3. b   4. c   5. b   6. b   7. c   8. a   9. d   10. c
11. d 12. d 13. d 14. d 15. d 16. a 17. d 18. a 19. d 20. a
21. d 22. d 23. b 24. c 25. c 26. c 27. d 28. d 29. a 30. d
31. d 32. b 33. c 34. b 35. d 36. d 37. d

Chapter 15
1. b   2. d   3. d   4. d   5. d   6. d   7. d   8. d   9. d   10. a
11. a 12. d 13. d 14. d 15. d 16. d 17. d 18. d 19. d 20. d
21. b 22. b 23. d 24. d 25. d 26. d 27. b 28. d 29. b 30. d
31. d 32. d 33. d 34. c 35. c 36. a 37. d 38. b 39. d 40. b
41. c 42. d 43. b 44. b 45. d 46. c 47. d 48. d 49. d 50. c

Chapter 16
1. d   2. d   3. d   4. d   5. d   6. c   7. d   8. d   9. d   10. d
11. d 12. d 13. c 14. d 15. d 16. b 17. d 18. a 19. d 20. a
21. d 22. d 23. d 24. a 25. d 26. d 27. d 28. d 29. d 30. b
31. d 32. a

Chapter 17
1. a   2. d   3. d   4. d   5. d   6. d   7. b   8. a   9. c   10. a
11. a 12. b 13. d 14. a 15. d 16. a 17. a 18. a 19. a

Chapter 18
1. c   2. b   3. d   4. d   5. b   6. c   7. a   8. b   9. d   10. b
11. c 12. d 13. b 14. d 15. c 16. d 17. d 18. a 19. d 20. d
21. d 22. c

Chapter 19
1. d   2. d   3. c   4. d   5. d   6. b   7. c   8. c   9. d

Chapter 20
1. d   2. b   3. a   4. b   5. d   6. b   7. a   8. b   9. d   10. b
11. d

Chapter 21
1. a   2. d   3. c   4. c   5. d   6. b   7. d   8. c   9. d   10. d
11. b

www.ingramcontent.com/pod-product-compliance
Lightning Source LLC
Chambersburg PA
CBHW082045230426
43670CB00016B/2782